Patrick
Leigh Fermor

# Patrick
# Leigh Fermor

NOBLE ENCOUNTERS
*between*
BUDAPEST *and* TRANSYLVANIA

Michael O'Sullivan

CEU PRESS

CENTRAL EUROPEAN UNIVERSITY PRESS
BUDAPEST–NEW YORK

Published in 2018 by
Central European University Press
Nádor utca 11, H-1051 Budapest, Hungary
*Tel:* +36-1-327-3138 or 327-3000   *Fax:* +36-1-327-3183
*E-mail:* ceupress@press.ceu.edu   *Website:* www.ceupress.com

224 West 57th Street, New York NY 10019, USA

ISBN  978-615-5225-64-2 paperback

**LIBRARY OF CONGRESS CATALOGING-IN-PUBLICATION DATA**
Names: O'Sullivan, Michael, 1957- author.
Title: Patrick Leigh Fermor : noble encounters between Budapest and
Transylvania / Michael O'Sullivan.
Description: Budapest ; New York : Central European University Press,
2018. | Includes bibliographical references and index.
Identifiers: LCCN 2018009070 (print) | LCCN 2018022873 (ebook) | ISBN
9789633861721 (pdf) | ISBN 9786155225642 (pbk. : alk. paper)
Subjects: LCSH: Fermor, Patrick Leigh--Travel--Hungary. | Fermor, Patrick
Leigh--Travel--Romania--Transylvania. | Hungary--Description and travel. |
Transylvania (Romania)--Description and travel. | Hungary--Social life and
customs--20th century. | Transylvania (Romania)--Social life and customs--
20th century.
Classification: LCC DB955.6.F47 (ebook) | LCC DB955.6.F47 O88 2018
(print) | DDC 943.905/1--dc23
LC record available at https://lccn.loc.gov/2018009070

Printed in Hungary by Prime Rate Kft.

*In memory of*
*Rudolf Fischer (1923–2016)*
*Mimi von Marquet (1918–2015)*
*Stella von Musulin (1915–1996)*

# Contents

*Titles may be inherited by blood, granted by a monarch or bought with money; nobility must be earned.*

Hungarian proverb

# Acknowledgements

I had the great benefit of meeting Patrick Leigh Fermor's Budapest mentor, Rudi Fischer, in the last years of his life, and, like Leigh Fermor, my debt to him is inestimable. I am also grateful to his wife Dagmar for her kind hospitality in Budapest. Two other great Hungarian friends of mine were stalwart supporters of the book from the outset and I can never be sufficiently effusive in my thanks for their unfailing help in response to my seemingly endless queries about the Hungarian nobility. Therefore my most sincere thanks go to János Mátyásfalvi and to Tom Barcsay de Nagybarcsa. János Mátyásfalvi gave me unrestricted access to his extraordinary private archive on the history of Budapest. My travels through Transylvania with Tom Barcsay were the single greatest source of inspiration for this book as I was privileged on those trips to tap into his unrivalled knowledge of the region of which his ancestor Ákos Barcsay was Prince and his great-uncle, Count Miklós Bánffy, was *primus inter pares* among Transylvania's most cultured noblemen. Prince Mark Odescalchi was unstinting in his generosity in answering my many queries about his family and he also kindly read the manuscript.

It gives me particular pleasure to thank the descendants of the many Hungarian noble families who gave Patrick Leigh Fermor hospitality in 1934 and whose extended family connections add to this story and who have also been equally generous to me over the many years of my association with their homeland. Baroness Gloria von Berg's father was the first Hungarian nobleman to accommodate Patrick Leigh Fermor in Hungary and I am very grateful to her for allowing me access to her family archives and photographs and for her great encouragement and friendship. Esther Ronay very kindly read the manuscript and saved me from many errors by her scrupulous attention to detail. All those which remain are entirely due to me alone.

The many others to whom I am very grateful include: Count István Pálffy ab Erdőd, Barbara Piazza-Georgi and her mother, Katharina Hunyor de Vizsoly, HRH Leka Crown Prince of Albania, Count József Hunyady de Kéthely and his wife, Countess Katalin Hunyady de Kéthely (née Almásy de Zsadány et Törökszentmiklós), the late Anna Sándor de Kénos, Miklós Klobusiczky de Klobusicz et Zétény (whose father Elemér or 'István' in *Between the Woods and the Water* was Leigh Fermor's closest Hungarian friend), Marquesa Zita Pallavicini, Catherine Dickens (whose grandfather Count Wenckheim was one of three Wenckheim counts who gave Leigh Fermor hospitality), Countess Teleki de Szék, Baron János Gudenus, Count Szapáry de Szapár Muraszombat et Széchy-Sziget, Stefania Betegh de Csiktusnád, János Wettstein von Westersheimb, Baroness Mhari Kemény and Eva Kiss. Princess Marianne Galitzine (whose family were exiled twice under Communism—from Russia and from Hungary) gave me a great sense of how those old noble families endured huge loss in the face of tyranny. I am also grateful to the late Deborah Dowager Duchess of Devonshire (and James Mullen for his kind introduction to her in London), Jaap Scholten, who gave me many kind introductions in Hungary, Manu von Marquet, who provided many memories of his Mother 'Mimi' Countess Maria Markovits von Spizza de Kisterpest, from whom I first heard of Patrick Leigh Fermor in 1982, and the late Baroness Stella von Musulin, to whom I owe so much of my knowledge of Central Eastern Europe ever since I was a young man living in Vienna.

Professor Norman Stone kindly read the manuscript and provided many hours of helpful and most enjoyable conversation about Hungarian history. Dr Ferenc Takács gave me the initial introductions to Rudi Fischer and to Leigh Fermor's Hungarian translator, the late Miklós Vajda. Professor István Pogány very kindly allowed me to read parts of his unpublished family memoir. I am grateful to David Pryce-Jones for a fascinating discussion we had in Budapest about Unity Mitford's relationship to Hungary. Irina Leca of that most excellent architectural archive in Bucharest, Monumente Uitate, was also most helpful. Tom Sawford is owed special mention for maintaining, through many years of devotion, the excellent website on PLF. Professor Attila Pók kindly facilitated my access to the the Hungarian State Security Archives.

Close personal friends of Hungarian descent were loyal supporters of the book *ab initio* and they include Klára Szakall von Losoncz, Ildiko Moran, András and Nora Újlaky. The author András Török was also most helpful as was my friend Sebo Kanat. My thanks also go to some of my dear friends, including Petroc Trelawny, Zeynep Asya Ostroumoff, Richard Bassett and Philip Mansel, Sissy and Goran Mornhed, Tom and Annabel Howells, who all gave regular encouragement when spirits were flagging.

I am also grateful to Patrick Leigh Fermor's biographer, Artemis Cooper, and to Joan Leigh Fermor's biographer, Simon Fenwick, and to David McClay at the National Library of Scotland where the Patrick Leigh Fermor archive is deposited. Finally I would like to thank the publisher, CEU Press, its staff and the director, Krisztina Kós who has been supportive and enthusiastic about the manuscript from the start.

# A Note on Personal Names, Place Names and Hungarian Titles

In the case of place names, I adhere to Leigh Fermor's own usage, thus: Rumania and not Romania etc. Likewise, I have used his favoured Constantinople rather than Istanbul throughout, mainly to avoid conflict in areas when I am quoting from *Between the Woods and the Water* and mention the city in my own text in the same paragraph. On the issue of pre–Treaty of Trianon place names in territories no longer under Hungarian suzerainty in 1934, again I follow Leigh Fermor's lead and certainly the custom of his hosts in Hungary and Transylvania at that time. I use the old Hungarian name and then give the post-Trianon name in parenthesis thus: Kolozsvár (Cluj). In very occasional instances I use the German place name usually when referring to a Saxon settlement in Transylvania.

With regard to Hungarian street names I employ the Hungarian not the English for street (*út, utca*), avenue/boulevard (*körút*), square (*tér*). In the Hungarian language family names are always given in the Eastern name order, the family name precedes that of the given name. I use the Western name order to avoid confusion for readers unaccustomed to the Hungarian practice. All Hungarian first names remain non-anglicized and given in their Hungarian original.

The issue of Hungarian aristocratic titles and the attendant issue of the term 'nobility' is a quagmire of genealogical confusion, even for Hungarians. In Hungary one may be noble but not titled. Those who in England would be considered untitled landed gentry are often of older lineage than many of the titled nobility. It is similar in Hungary. Many landed untitled families were of more ancient and distinguished lineage than those who received titles of nobility under the Habsburgs. The last Habsburg King of Hungary, Charles IV, bestowed the last title of nobility in 1918. Then there are also the ancient Hungarian titles and this area itself is very much more complicated than this brief attempt at simplification allows. From the thirteenth century the Hungarian King bestowed titles of nobility which had hereditary effect. The title of Prince of Transylvania did not carry such hereditary status, thus families such as the Barcsay de Nagybarcsa, though of ancient lineage and once princes of Transylvania, carry no style or title preceding their name.

I follow the *Almanach de Gotha*'s rule of prefix and therefore most titles are rendered with 'von' and 'de', except in the case of Pálffy ab Erdőd, which (through usage that extends back to the sixteenth century) should always appear in this form.

In the case of the upper echelons of the Hungarian nobility, there were only a very limited number of families who intermarried and in many instances first cousins wed. The Hungarian nobility adhered to an almost primal endogamy when it came to marriage matches. This can make the task of attempting to fathom who *exactly* one is looking at in a family tree something of an uphill struggle at times. Therefore, when referring to some of Leigh Fermor's hosts in Hungary, the Banat and Transylvania I sometimes give a string of Christian names to avoid possible confusion with another family member of the same first name. I beg the reader's indulgence on this matter.

Finally, all Hungarian and even foreign titles of nobility granted to Hungarians were abolished in Hungary in 1947 under Statute Number IV of that year. The legislation was introduced by the Communist-dominated government of the post-war Republic of 1946–49 and declares 'the abolition, and prohibition of use, of all hereditary noble ranks and related styles and titles'. Having sequestered all the land and property and personal possessions of the nobility, the Communist state was determined on the ultimate humiliation of these 'class enemies' by removing their last remaining incorporeal hereditament. There have been several attempts in Hungary to revoke the legislation—even as recently as 2011. Despite these efforts, it still remains on the statute books with full effect. However, one still occasionally hears in Budapest and elsewhere in Hungary, the age-old Hungarian courtesy greeting, so often heard by Patrick Leigh Fermor in 1934: '*Jó estét, kedves grófnő, kezét csókolom*' (Good evening, dear Countess, I kiss your hand).

# Introduction

*It is not true that fate slips silently into our lives.*
*It steps in through the door that we have opened,*
*and we invite it to enter.*

Sándor Márai, *Embers*

Patrick Leigh Fermor was completely unaware on a cold Easter day in March 1934 as he crossed the Mária Valéria Bridge from Czechoslovakia into Hungary at Esztergom, that he would one day become the chronicler of a form of social life and of a class, which were soon to be extinguished by the vicissitudes of war, the repression which was so often the attendant handmaiden of Communism and in some cases by their own folly.

From the moment he set foot on Hungarian soil he fell into the welcoming embrace of a significant number of some of the oldest and grandest families in the land. This poorly dressed, slightly dishevelled, nineteen-year-old traveller, speaking English, schoolboy French and basic German, soon found himself associating with two Habsburg Archdukes, a former Hungarian Prime Minister and Foreign Minister, a Cardinal Archbishop, the King of Rumania's Master of the Hunt, a Hungarian Princess, a Marquessa, Counts and Countesses, Barons and Baronesses, landed squires and ennobled diplomats. Or as he once put it himself, 'people whose families were ancient when God was a boy'. He stayed for much of that time in the castles and manor houses of this former ruling elite, some of whom could trace their lineage back a thousand years. How did this unknown young man find himself in this position?

Much has been made of the fact that he also slept in hay barns, shepherds' huts and under the stars. This is quite true for other parts of his journey from the Hook of Holland to Constantinople, but during his time in Hungary, the Banat and Transylvania, which is the part explored in this book, he was rarely without the use of a comfortable bed in some castle or manor house. The book examines the time he spent with these ancient families, many of whose names still mark the streets, squares and roads on which Leigh Fermor walked in 1934. It looks at the history of these families and at the often complex history of the politics of the period, during which he stayed with them. Was it simple good fortune or fate which saw this extraordinary young man entering the lives of these families?

It begins with his lengthy stay in Budapest, where he was given accommodation by the dashing, handsome adventurer and Anglophile, Baron Tibor von Berg, who had made a journey in part similar to the journey Leigh Fermor was then setting out on. Von Berg had gone on horseback from Budapest to Constantinople in 1926. Leigh Fermor interacted with these aristocrats with such easy and intimate affability that in later years he would become one of their most memorable limners. Where possible I use interviews with surviving members of these old families with whom he stayed. I have also tried to ascertain the fate of many of these families quite soon after his departure from their lives, when the old order was quite suddenly, and often rather brutally, changed forever. I have recorded, where possible, what physically happened to many of the houses in which Leigh Fermor stayed after Hungary and Rumania became Soviet satellite states.

Why was a wandering English youth, who had been expelled from school at the age of sixteen, so frequently accommodated with such ease among this ancient magnate class? Breaching the fortified social ha-has of the ascendancy in any society has never been easily achieved. That it should be achieved by a nineteen-year-old, unknown English middle-class *peregrinus* has, for decades, puzzled enthusiasts and detractors alike, of the later internationally renowned author. His address list at the back of a diary he kept at this period reads like a series of entries from the *Almanach de Gotha*. Every name, with few exceptions, is prefixed by an aristocratic title. What Leigh Fermor offered these old families made him particularly welcome in this part of the former Austro-Hungarian Empire. He was then, as he would remain throughout his life, a curious cocktail of geniality and genealogy. He had a natural interest in, and curiosity about, the history of these ancient families. He had charm and good manners. To the old he was attentive and polite; to the young he was exciting and handsome.

But there was another reason why he was found to be so socially acceptable to these ancient families and that involved some duplicity, however unintended it may have been on his part. It was not simply a matter, as he himself presents it, of the aristocratic Hungarians liking the English or the rarity value of his journey, which saw him so readily accommodated in the castles of Hungary. There was nothing rapacious in this youthful engagement with snobbery or with his claims of an ancient Irish noble ancestry however dubious those claims may have been. From his earliest days he bestrode the lives of the grand and the ordinary, coasting along quite comfortably in each but never quite knowing which group he favoured most or to which he really belonged. Ultimately, he was self-assured enough not to really care about such things. Likewise he never really sought out fame for fame's sake but rather followed

Keats's advice to those seeking it: 'Make your best bow to her and bid adieu; / Then if she likes it, she will follow you.'

Suspending disbelief when reading Leigh Fermor is sometimes not just useful but often a *sine qua non*. This remark is in no way intended as a discordant note meant to detract from his consummate skill as one of the great prose stylists of his generation. Lawrence Durrell rightly referred to the 'truffled style and dense plumage' of his marvellous prose. There is throughout his writing, the sense of the world as a place full of infinite wonder and variety and of his desire to know as much about it as possible. His writing is often all the better for engaging the occasional *madeleine* rather than always relying on hard fact. *Se non è vero...* Dervla Murphy is most astute in her assessment of this side of his writing when she wrote: 'it doesn't matter a damn whether he is describing it as he remembers it in 1934 or in 1964 or simply as he fancies it might have been in 1634'. A man who could write with such finely tuned historical understanding of the significance of the 'discord' of the church bells of Kolozsvár (Cluj), describing them with piercing accuracy as being 'reciprocally schismatic' can surely be afforded more than an occasional dash of poetic licence. All the more so because he didn't set foot in the place until 1982. This view is also supported by his biographer, Artemis Cooper, who knew him well as a friend and as a subject for scholarship. George Szirtes, though not writing specifically about Leigh Fermor, put the condition most elegantly: 'One invents everything: the world, one's friends and lovers and family, every power one is bound to and, most of all, oneself. Then one has to believe all these inventions and act in the world they inhabit.'

Though we had a few friends in common, unfortunately I never met Patrick Leigh Fermor. Therefore I do not feel entitled or comfortable using what I consider to be the over-familiar 'Paddy' and instead use the impersonal 'Leigh Fermor' throughout the text. I hope that this will be accepted, as it is intended, as a mark of respect. He was using the name Michael during his time in Hungary; also sometimes even practicing writing variants of his surname in the back of his diary in 1934. He seemed a little unsure as to whether it should be hyphenated or not or whether he should be at times Michael or Patrick or Paddy. In the only two extant guest books, from his 1934 journey, at least after extensive searches for any others, the only two I have been able to thus far locate, he signs himself as 'Michael Leigh Fermor'. His replacement passport issued in Munich on January 15, 1934, was signed by the bearer in the form 'Michael Leigh-Fermor' even though his birth certificate registration lists him as 'Fermor, Patrick M.' and the passport was issued to 'Patrick Michael Leigh Fermor'. But this was all part of the rich tapestry which went to make up the fascinating character who will forever be known to his legion of friends and followers endearingly as 'Paddy'.

His life-long indenture to the pen and to the imagination sustained his very individual sense of the truth but it was an apprenticeship not without its own torments. Self-doubt as to his ability to sustain his writing skill was a source of anguish frequently attending him in what Auden liked to call the writer's 'cave of making'. It also does no harm to remember that this sublime prose stylist was also, *primus inter pares*, a consummate performer.

There are also contentious issues which Leigh Fermor aficionados will be aware of and which I hope to shed new light on. These are the questions of his apparent lack of interest in the explosive political period in which he travelled; his romantic tryst with a married Hungarian aristocratic woman and also whether or not he made the now legendary car journey across Transylvania with her which occupies the chapter in *Between the Woods and the Water* entitled 'Triple Fugue'. There is also the issue of his doubtful noble Irish ancestry with its connection to Austria-Hungary and the part this played in the success of his Hungarian journey. I examine the background of the Irish noble family from whom his mother claimed to be descended. In doing so I hope to remove him from under the carapace of genealogical myth created by her very febrile imagination.

This book is also, in considerable part, a portrait of Budapest at a particularly interesting time in its history. It was a city on the very cusp of momentous change when Leigh Fermor visited it in 1934.

I first heard of Patrick Leigh Fermor when I was a young man living in Vienna in the early 1980s. The conversation about him, which I overheard at a party in a Hungarian friend's flat, had nothing to do with his books or his life as a soldier, war hero and adventurer. *Between the Woods and the Water* had not yet been published, so there was, at that time, no comprehensive public knowledge of his journey through Hungary, the Banat and Transylvania during the 'Great Trudge', as he later liked to call it. No one in those days, except perhaps for a few intimates and a handful of survivors from among his Magyar encounters, knew very much about this section of his journey or the people he met from the point where he crossed the Danube at Esztergom. *A Time of Gifts*, the first volume of a proposed trilogy, dealt with the earlier leg of the journey, and ended with the fervent promise to the reader that the story was 'To Be Continued'. It has been my wish for some time now to continue the story a little further to ensure those who were in themselves often fascinating people in Hungary the Banat and Transylvania and who were kind to a wandering English youth would also not be forgotten.

The source of my first intelligence and curiosity about Patrick Leigh Fermor and Hungary at that Vienna party was one of those Central European aristocratic women in exile from her homeland. She was of a type immortalized in *Between the Woods and the Water*, the second volume of the trilogy, which was published in 1986. The Hungarian Countess Maria Markovits von Spizza de Kisterpest (Mrs Max von Marquet and known to her friends as Mimi (1918–2014)) had gathered around her a group of English-speaking expatriates whom she was regaling with stories of 'a dashing young Englishman who walked to Istanbul in 1934' and who had stayed in the castles of some of her friends in Hungary. By one of those curious coincidences her family had a house in the same street where Leigh Fermor was accommodated in Budapest in 1934. My interest was sufficiently aroused to start asking questions about this wandering Aengus.

I had the great good fortune to know a friend of W.H. Auden's—who was the scholarly purpose for my being in Austria at that time—and who lived at Ober-Grafendorf, outside Vienna, and whom I felt was likely to know something of this exotic Englishman. The writer and historian Stella Musulin (Baroness von Musulin de Gomirje, née Lloyd-Philipps of Dale) had become something of a mentor to me during my Vienna years and it was to her that I turned for information on Leigh Fermor's stay in Hungary and Transylvania. Stella, too, like her friend, Mimi von Marquet, knew some of the Hungarian aristocrats with whose families he had been hospitably billeted during his walk. She also knew some of the people he had met on his earlier progress through Austria. She was familiar with *A Time of Gifts* and described it as 'sublime' and added that she was 'longing to read the next instalment'. Over the next few years Stella introduced me to some of her Hungarian aristocratic friends who had fled Hungary in 1944 when the Nazis were in control of Budapest, and to some of those who had left in 1956 when the Hungarian Revolution offered an opportunity to flee the brutal Stalinist regime of Mátyás Rákosi.

Thus began my personal involvement with some of these old Hungarian families who, though then rather necessitous when it came to worldly goods, were rich in family history, and, above all, in an admirable sense of dignity in the face of tremendous loss. There was an allure about these people, which made them for me something other than down-at-heel princelings remembering the phantoms of their quondam ascendancy.

The impetus to write the book finally came when I met Leigh Fermor's Budapest mentor, Rudi Fischer. It is quite clear from over 400 letters between Leigh Fermor and Fischer during and after the writing of *Between the Woods and the Water* that his debt to him was, as he put it in his generous acknowledgement, 'inestimable'. Rudi Fischer was a pedagogue of the old school; a Transylvanian Saxon whose knowledge of the region was profound. Without him *Between the Woods and the Water* would, as Leigh Fermor readily admitted, have been a rather different book.

I first visited Budapest in 1982, the same year in which I had heard talk of Leigh Fermor at that party in Vienna. It has taken me many years to get around to this much-neglected subject which forms the central part of one of his most esteemed books—those old Hungarian families he met 'between the woods and the water' in 1934. I hope that in finally doing so I have been equitable in my assessment of them and of him.

Prologue

# The Bridge at Esztergom

*A journey is always a rescue operation, the documentation and harvesting of something that is becoming extinct and will soon disappear.*

Claudio Magris, *Danube*

Easter Saturday 1934. The city of Esztergom is en fête as the religious ceremonies which mark the end of the Lenten period of abstinence get underway. An English youth, expelled from the King's School, Canterbury, two years earlier, for being caught holding hands with the very pretty daughter of a local greengrocer and diagnosed at this time by his housemaster as 'a dangerous mixture of sophistication and recklessness', walks across the frontier which divides Czechoslovakia from Hungary. Regardless of a capricious March wind gusting up the Danube, he pauses for a lengthy period on the bridge which spans the river between Párkány (Štúrovo) on the Czechoslovak side and Hungary's archiepiscopal seat at Esztergom on the river's right bank. Patrick Michael Leigh Fermor was of slight build, 5 foot, 9 inches, in height, had brown wavy hair with a permanent cow's lick in front and dark brown eyes. He was strikingly handsome and his bearing was both confident and impressive for one so young. He had only recently celebrated his nineteenth birthday while undertaking a most unusual walk from the Hook of Holland to Constantinople, as he always favoured calling the city which had been named Istanbul in 1930, when the munic-

9

ipality's postal service ceased delivering mail addressed to 'Constantinople'.

His motivation for this now legendary 'Great Trudge', as he later referred to it, was a mixture of thwarted literary ambition, combined with parental pressure to abandon the dissipated life he was leading in London. He saw himself at this time as "tormented by restlessness and longing to escape". Adventure was also in his blood. His father, Lewis Leigh Fermor, had left behind a suburban background in England to join the Geological Survey of India at the age of twenty-two. The young Patrick, or Michael as he was remembered by some of the family members of friends he made on this part of his journey, was aware that even his schooling had been something of a disappointment to his parents. His father had hoped for him to be educated at a school where science was taken seriously in an era when a classical education was still perceived to be important in the formation of a gentleman. His mother, whose snobbery knew few bounds, wished for her son to be schooled at Eton, which produced many of England's ruling elite. The King's School, Canterbury, was an educational institution of great antiquity which numbers writers such as Christopher Marlowe and W. Somerset Maugham among its old boys, however, it can claim few great statesmen among their number.

Youthful self-loathing also played no small part in his decision to undertake the adventure. A perfunctory attempt at cramming for the military academy at Sandhurst was more enthusiastically coupled with partying with the remnants of the generation of Bright Young Things, until he could no longer tolerate or indeed afford this lifestyle. In a moment of confessional self-analysis he wrote: '[A] sudden loathing of London. Everything [...] seeming loathsome, trivial, restless, shoddy [...] detestation, suddenly, of parties. Contempt for everyone, starting and finishing with myself.' He set off during the second week of December, 1933, with a sparsely packed rucksack, carrying an edition of Horace's *Odes* in which his mother had inscribed a quotation from Petronius which could hardly have been more apt for such an adventure: 'Leave thy home, O youth, and seek out alien shores. [...] Yield not to misfortune: the far-off Danube shall know thee.' He embarked on this journey, without any preconceptions or prejudices, his mind something of a *tabula rasa*, the most perfect instrument for recording the adventures which lay ahead.

It was three years since his expulsion from school and three months into the journey which had thus far taken him on foot through the Netherlands, Germany, Austria, and Czechoslovakia. Now as he stood on the Mária Valéria Bridge at Esztergom he was, quite understandably, unaware

The Bridge at Esztergom, about 1934 (later bombed during WW II).
The Basilica is to the left in the photograph

that what he was contemplating was the exhilarating intoxication of the last remaining years of old *Mitteleuropa*. He was also unaware that he was about to become a witness to a way of life which would soon be doomed and eliminated.

The austere neo-classical façade of the basilica at Esztergom dominates this stretch of the Danube some sixty-five kilometres from Budapest. In the so-called 'Green Diary', a contemporary account he kept sporadically during the walk, he tells us quite simply, 'my first impression of Hungary was good'. His first impression of the basilica, perched on a hill on the other side of the Danube, was it somehow looked 'oriental'. Leigh Fermor could hardly have chosen a more symbolic point of entry into Hungary than this attractive riverside town. For it was here that Géza, father of Hungary's Stephen I, king and saint, established his court and here too is the place where Stephen chose to embrace Western Catholicism rather than Eastern Orthodoxy and to banish the pagan practices of old.

Soon after crossing the bridge he made his way to the centre of Esztergom as the crisp effervescence of the Danube light was failing. He noticed the windows of most of the houses were illuminated by votive candles, the combined effect, from a distance, casting a gentle and welcoming light. He felt, in this ancient place, all the omens were good for the journey which lay ahead. When he reached the area at the foot of the great basilica he produced the first of many letters of introduction he had been given for members of some of Hungary's old families. A friendly encounter with a policeman prompted him to produce from his rucksack a letter for the Mayor of Esztergom, Dr Gyula Glatz. He gratifyingly recalls in his diary how 'impressed the policeman was with this letter'. He gives us an indication of his own nascent snobbery when he notes the officer told him that 'the Mayor was married to a Baroness'. It may have pleased him even more had the officer been in a position to tell him the Mayor was married to a Baroness of Hiberno-Norman descent. Dr Glatz had married Baroness Izabella Butler, whose family settled in Ireland in the twelfth century and whose descendants later gave distinguished service to the Habsburg Empire in both military and political roles. Descended from the Earls of Ossory and Dukes of Ormond, a Butler baroness was perfect stock to add to the rapidly expanding *Almanac* of grandees he was keeping at the back of his diary. The baroness was a kinswoman of James Butler, first Duke of Ormond, who was instrumental in inviting Huguenots to settle in Ireland after the revocation of the Edict of Nantes. Her kinsman knew the deprivations of exile having spent many years as part of the Irish diaspora in France after the failure of his attempts to lead the Irish and Royalist forces to defeat Oliver Cromwell. At this stage of his journey, Leigh Fermor's own doubtful claim to be of ancient noble Irish lineage was something of a *vade mecum* and was to be become, as we shall see, a trump card played though not with any intended duplicity throughout much of his journey in Hungary and beyond.

After his introduction to Dr Glatz he moved with the mayoral party, consisting of the nobility, city burghers, the clergy and the Prince-Primate of Hungary, Cardinal Jusztinián György Serédi, to gather in front of the basilica. He noted once more, in a favourite description of his in those youthful days, the 'oriental' look of the nobles' uniforms. The nobleman who escorted him 'carried his scimitar slung nonchalantly in the crook of his arm' and polished his rimless eyeglass with equal nonchalance using a coloured silk bandana. The Cardinal, who was also Archbishop of Esztergom, was about to lead the Easter ceremonies in the imposingly named Primatial Basilica of the Blessed Virgin Mary Assumed into Heaven and St Adalbert. Much to his surprise, Leigh Fermor was included in the mayoral party and swept along in its wake through the granite portal of the great edifice and seated in a place of honour near the altar.

Cardinal Serédi and the Mayor of Esztergom in the 1930s

In Esztergom Leigh Fermor noted the power, pomp and ritual of the Catholic Church. Many among the assembled citizens, from peasant to aristocrat, fell on one knee, as was the custom of the time, to kiss the archiepiscopal ring and also to pay homage to the Blessed Sacrament as it was carried through the streets in a golden monstrance under a heavily embroidered canopy supported by four sumptuously uniformed Hungarian noblemen. He had a perfect vantage point at the front of the basilica to view the thurifers incensing the faithful and to hear the long traditional Easter ceremonial rites being read. The Cardinal's homily, in Hungarian, would certainly have been lengthy and dealt principally with the Passion of Christ but Cardinal Serédi, at this time, was a somewhat controversial and often outspoken figure, and his remarks are quite likely to have contained some important, if diplomatically veiled references, to contemporary political events.

The year of Leigh Fermor's arrival in Hungary, the Cardinal issued a statement urging his clergy not to support the principles of Nazism. However, as a member of Hungary's upper house of parliament, he voted in favour of anti-Semitic legislation. Later, in 1939 when over 150,000 Polish refugees, including thousands of Jews, arrived in Hungary he did much to help them, including arranging a school and temporary foster homes for the Jewish children. Ten years, almost to the day on which Leigh Fermor encountered him, in April 1944, while protesting against the treatment of Jews by the Nazis and by Hungarian fascists, he also protested at the deportation of baptized Hungarian Jews. However, he was reluctant to extend his protest to include all Jews, fearing that to do so would merely expedite rather than halt their deportation. The Cardinal, a modest man, was always mindful of his own humble peasant origins— the Church and the Army were two vehicles for social preferment in Hungary in those days when the aristocracy and the upper middle class still held a monopoly on power and social privilege. His predecessor Cardinal Csernoch, a Slovak, was from a similar social background. It was he who crowned Charles IV as the last King of Hungary in 1916. The nineteen-year-old Leigh Fermor was embarking, that Easter day, on the first of a series of remarkable meetings with some of the most influential people in Hungary.

After a one-night stay, which included dinner at the Mayor's house, where he met this gentleman's titled wife who, to his great delight, spoke English, he wondered if 'all of Hun-

"Mimi" Countess Maria Markovits von Spizza de Kisterpest

gary could be like this?' He slept the first evening in a hotel room paid for by the Mayor from where he confessed to his diary 'the Hungarians certainly seem to be grand people and very hospitable'. The first acknowledgement on the written page of what would become something of a weakness of his but also a confirmation of his limitless capacity to charm—living high on the hog without having the personal means to do so. The next day, refusing a lift in a Bugatti, the young traveller walked south through the verdant terrain offered him by the gently undulating landscape of the Pilis and Visegrád hills; moving on through 'the little tearful-sounding town of Szob', then Visegrád and finally sleepy elegant eighteenth-century Szentendre, then onward towards Budapest. 'Little remains of the journey from Szentendre: a confused impression of cobbled approaches, the beginnings of tramlines, some steep streets and airy views of the Danube and its bridges and the search for the hill of Buda' is how he recalls it in *Between the Woods and the Water*.

Szentendre provided a rural haven for artists seeking to avoid urban life in Budapest and an artists' colony was es-

PLF's father Sir Lewis Leigh Fermor

tablished here in the early twentieth century. In his haste to reach Budapest he leaves us with just a brief mention of these places on the way. Szentendre he describes as 'a little baroque country town of lanes, cobbled streets, tiled roofs and belfries with onion cupolas. The hills were lower now; vineyards and orchards had replaced the cliffs and the forests and there was a feeling in the air that one was nearing a great city. The townspeople were the descendants of Serbs who had fled from the Turks three centuries ago; they still talked Serbian and worshipped in the Greek Orthodox Cathedral which their ancestors had built'.

His approach to Budapest brought him over the *Rózsadomb* (*Gültepe*, or 'Rose Hill' in Turkish), where remnants of Ottoman Buda still survive to this day. He carried on down through the *Víziváros* or Watertown, where the ancient Király baths were and still are located, another reminder of Ottoman times, finally making his descent to the *Vár* or Castle district. Here he spent twelve memorable days which would prove to be a combination of his favourite cocktail, a heady mixture of the sybaritic and the cerebral.

Vor meiner Südamerikafahrt, mit vielen Dank
u. der Hoffnung auf ein gesundes, frohes
Wiedersehen!
2. April 34.

Günther Frhr. v. Berg
der singende Vetter aus Brasilien

Michael Leigh-Fermor
28 Market Street,
Berkeley Square
W. 1.

Mayfair 0225.

Budapest, April 1934.

Francis Hotham
52 Chester Terrace
Eaton Sq. S.W 1.

Gróf Bem de Kisbán
Budapest 1934.V.8

PLF's signature as 'Michael' in the von Berg's Guestbook, 1934

I

# Budapest

*Budapest is a prime site for dreams: the East's exuberant vision of the West,*
*the West's uneasy hallucination of the East.*

Claudio Magris, *Danube*

Leigh Fermor's destination once he reached the Hungarian capital on April 1 was a house at 15 Úri utca, right in the heart of Buda's *Vár* or castle quarter. 'A waving street of jutting windows, tiled roofs and arched doors with coats of arms' was his first observation of this medieval Buda streetscape. His first nights there attest to the generosity of his hosts Baron Tibor and Baroness Berta von Berg, as indeed does his enthusiastic description of one of his first mornings waking up in their house. The previous evening's hectic social activities left him with temporary alcohol-induced amnesia and when he woke up he was at a loss to know where exactly he was. The sudden smell of freshly brewed coffee brought him to his senses. That comforting aroma and the appearance in his bedroom of the twelve-year-old Micky von Berg bearing a silver tray with curative Alka Seltzer and coffee soon brought him to an awareness of his location. The presence of Micky's energetic dog jumping on the bed looking for someone to play with had a less calming effect. He recalls looking up at a vaulted ceiling in a room in which hundreds of books seemed to cover every surface and tumble from every niche and 'across the arms of a chair embroidered with a blue rampant lion with a forked tail and a scarlet tongue, a dinner jacket was untidily thrown. An evening tie hung from the looking glass, pumps lay in different corners, the crumpled torso of a stiff shirt (still worn with a black tie in those days) gesticulated desperately across the carpet and borrowed links glittered in the cuffs. The sight of all this alien plumage, so unlike the travel-stained heap that normally met my waking eyes, was a sequence of conundrums.' The auspices were still reading well for good days ahead.

Leigh Fermor's billet at 15 Úri utca was a convenient location from which to make forays around historic Budapest. The very name of the street was a harbinger of things to come. Úri utca translates as 'the street of the Lords' and it was in the company of such titled folk that he would spend the majority of his remaining time in Hungary and Transylvania. He was given free reign of an elegant vaulted-ceilinged guest room on the ground floor of number 15. Here he could come and go at all hours without disturbing the family on the upper floor. The von Bergs were his first up-close encounter with the many Hungarian aristocratic families who were to offer him hospitality as he made his way from Budapest to Constantinople and they did not prove a disappointment. They also set the pattern for what was to become a familiar part of the journey which lay ahead. The *paterfamilias* was a military man of considerable distinction. Tibor von Berg was a highly decorated veteran of the Great War in which he had been a cavalry officer. Before the war he worked in merchant banking in London for three years. After the war he built a boat on the Danube, which he called *Liberty* and he sailed around on her for a few years before finally returning to the army as an artillery officer and keen polo player. He had Irish Quaker blood and was descended from Christopher Pennock of Clonmel, County Tipperary, who emigrated to Pennsylvania around 1685. Tibor's grandmother, Sally-Mae Price, an heiress to

PLF in his youth

the Harlan and Hollingsworth shipbuilding fortune of Delaware and Pennsylvania, instilled in her grandson her Irish Quaker values. Leigh Fermor's own claim to Irish blood made him doubly welcome in the von Berg household. Tibor's daughter, Gloria, remembers her father as a 'liberal thinker who lived a slightly parsimonious life, completely unbothered by class distinctions and as someone who was anxious to impart these values to his children'. During his London years the young Baron was in the habit of taking his elderly English housekeeper to afternoon tea on Sundays, something which rather shocked some of the smart London cosmopolitan set in which he moved in those days. He was the type of man whom Leigh Fermor, lacking in paternal influence in his own life, looked up to throughout his journey. Also Leigh Fermor must have been fascinated and encouraged to discover that von Berg had made a similar journey to the one he was now undertaking.

In 1926, just eight years prior to Leigh Fermor's arrival in Budapest, Tibor von Berg, at the age of twenty-six, made the 1,340-kilometre journey from Budapest to Constantin-

Baron Tibor von Berg in the 1930s

ople on horseback. The twenty-five day journey took him from Budapest to Szeged, Makó, Apatfalva, on into Rumania's Temesvár (Timişoara), Mehadia, Calafat, onward to Bulgaria and Vidin, Berkovica, Sofia, Plovdiv, crossing into Turkey at Adrianople (Edirne in Turkish), finishing his ride at Çorlu in Thrace, where he had to sell his horse for what he describes as 'military reasons', some throwback, no doubt, to the Balkan wars. From here he took the train to Constantinople, just as Leigh Fermor would be forced to do at the end of his journey in 1935. 'I awaited with curiosity', the journalist Andor Medriczky writes in the Hungarian newspaper *Magyarság* on Saturday, July 24, 1926, about his appointment with von Berg in a hotel by the Bosphorus:

> I expected to find a tall muscle-bound individual with a fierce mustache, at least this is the way we imagine a bold horseman heads for Balkan forests and impenetrable roads on his own. [...] And now Baron Tibor Berg sits opposite me—young, mustacheless whose brown eyes radiate warmth with a touchingly youthful genuine sparkle lacking any hint of fatigue or of wild energy. His clothes are light and sporty of a kind one might wear on a ride from Budapest to Székesfehérvár.

It must surely have been singularly inspiring for Leigh Fermor to be in the company of such a man and to hear stories from a similar journey which he himself was about to

Micky von Berg in 1934

undertake. It is surprising that he makes no reference to it in *Between the Woods and the Water*. It appears everyone to whom von Berg mentioned the journey prior to leaving tried to discourage him from making it, mentioning export permits for his horse, and every other obstacle real or imagined that they could think of. Leigh Fermor received similar discouragement from the outset and indeed many times during his own journey. Von Berg made the journey in twenty-five days after obtaining the necessary travel documents. He travelled light, without even a change of clothes save for some fresh underwear in his saddle bag together with a revolver. Leigh Fermor too would later be armed with a pistol for his journey but in somewhat more curious circumstances. '[When] I started out on the great trip,' von Berg told the journalist, 'I had neither a map or compass with me.' Unfortunately von Berg never wrote about his experience but his verbal account of what he saw indicates powers of observation not dissimilar to the young Leigh Fermor's:

> The picture is one of variety and contrasts. After the tremendous agricultural prosperity of the Banat, that of the Regat seems poor, underdeveloped and unambitious. Neglect and lack of care everywhere. And then Bulgaria which is incomparably more modern, more orderly and has far better roads. Turkey, it is only now awakening from its centuries-old slumber. [...] [T]oday there are still ruins everywhere and its once-famous roads are overgrown with grass; a few old milestones remain here and there which I was able to use as guideposts. The people? Apart from a tiny minority, they were tremendously helpful—very interested in me but most of all they praised my horse. Let's face it, the Hungarian horse has no equal.

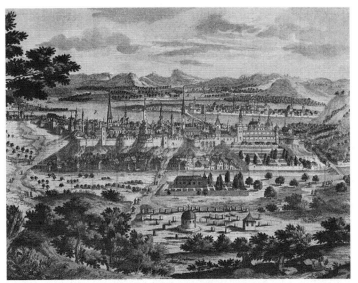

Buda, capital of the Eyalet or Province of Budin

It was propitious that Leigh Fermor, a nineteen-year-old interested in history, on his way to Constantinople on foot, should pitch up in a house in Budapest where he found a host completely sympathetic to what he was undertaking. It was also appropriate, given his final destination, that he should be staying in a place once occupied by the Ottomans. *Hisar peçe* was the Turkish name for this ancient area of Buda and it was from here the Turks ruled what they called the *Eyalet of Budin*, an administrative division within the Ottoman Empire. This gives, perhaps, at least some credence to the notion that the Orient begins not in Vienna, as Prince Metternich would have it, but further east, in Budapest. 'Budapest is a prime site for dreams: the East's exuberant vision of the West, the West's uneasy hallucination of the East,' is how Claudio Magris exquisitely puts it in *Danube*. It is on the west bank of the Danube, in Buda, where the few remaining traces of Ottoman Budapest are still evi-

dent. Leigh Fermor visited the tomb of the mystical dervish
Gül Baba, who is believed to have met his end in Buda during the first Ottoman religious victory ceremony held following their taking of the city in 1541. Perhaps an inappropriate way for a saint to meet his maker but so the legend
goes. His tomb is still a site of Muslim pilgrimage and devotion today. 'It seems, at moments, something of a fluke that
St Peter's and Notre Dame and Westminster Abbey are not
today three celebrated mosques, kindred fanes to Haghia
Sophia in Constantinople,' Leigh Fermor later observes in
contemplation of what might have become of Ottoman influence in Europe had the Turks successfully breached the
walls of Vienna in 1683.

It is also on the Buda side of the Danube where the remaining traces of Roman occupation of the ancient province of Pannonia are to be found. The empires of the Romans, the Ottoman Turks and Austro-Hungarians were
indeed entirely disparate institutions and it is not easy to
find many shared common connecting factors among them,
however, in Buda they found one common ground. The ancient springs under Buda provided a natural and constant
supply of water for the shared obsession all three had for
bathing. Buda still has functioning reminders of baths from
Ottoman times. Leigh Fermor also visited the site called
Aquincum, where he saw the ruins of the ancient Roman
baths. He was accompanied by the von Bergs' son Micky
(Miklós) and 'a beautiful girl of about fourteen called Harry, part Croatian and part Polish as well as Hungarian'.
The girl was Harry Kochanowsky, the half-sister of Ilona
Edelsheim who was married to the Regent Horthy's son
István. The party was accompanied by Micky's dog; 'an
Alsatian called Tim' (Gloria von Berg recalls a Doberman
called Edda) who foraged for bones among the ancient ru-

ins as the others admired a bas-relief of Mithras going about his gory sacrificial business of tauroctony—the slitting of a bull's throat. In the Roman relief a dog is seen jumping up to lick the bull's blood. Here, he observed, was the last bastion of ancient Rome 'for the Empire stopped at the river's

Gróf Széchenyi Lánchíd or Chain Bridge connecting Buda and Pest (1930s)

Kálvin tér in Pest as PLF would have seen it in 1934.
The Elizabeth fountain was still in place

bank'. These old demarcations of Empire still raise pride in the bosoms of visitors. Many years ago, standing with a Turkish friend on the Ferenc József Bridge, she paused looking downriver towards Csepel Island and then up at ancient Buda and with a plaintive sigh said, 'to think that this was once the frontier of our old Empire'.

Leigh Fermor makes it quite clear in his account of the city that he favoured Buda over Pest. The two city divisions and their ancient and often forgotten Cinderella portion of the ternion, Óbuda, formed a convenient and sensible union in 1873, though curiously Count István Széchenyi, the father of the Hungarian Academy and the man considered to this day to be 'the greatest Hungarian', refers to the city as 'Buda-Pest' as early as 1831 in a book of his entitled *Világ* (World). Széchenyi was the chief instigator of the construction of the first bridge to unite Buda and Pest, which was completed in 1849. Until then the citizens of the two distinct entities crossed the Danube by ferries subject to the vicissitudes of weather, on perilous floating pontoons or even more perilously still, on foot on the frozen ice in mid-winter. In the winter of 1820 it had taken Széchenyi a week to cross the river to attend his father's funeral. Thirty years later, the first bridge to link the two metropolitan areas, which would later unite to form one of Europe's great capitals, bore the name of the man inconvenienced by bad weather in attending his father's funeral.

Leigh Fermor tells us he never tired of viewing Pest from the vantage point known as the *Halászbástya*, the Fisherman's Bastion. This curious amalgam of neo-Gothic and neo-Romanesque architecture seems like a place of great antiquity but was completed only about thirty years before he arrived in Budapest. 'Architectural dash could scarcely go further' is his description of this splendid cut-stone belvedere.

Of Pest he held not so much a low opinion, but rather saw it as a place of modernity, with 'great Oxford Streets [...] slicing their canyons through the boom city'. He incorrectly dismissed it with his youthful eyes in the way a more seasoned antiquarian might not have done as: 'a place which only came into existence in the last century'. Though it is true to say as late as the early 1930s great swathes of Pest were still being developed and monuments both sec-

View from the *Halászbástya*, the Fisherman's Bastion, near the von Berg house (1934)

ular and sacred were being erected, much of it had a more ancient pedigree. But modernity was the order of the day for Pest in 1934 and he would have noted this as he ambled about this side of the city. Three years before Leigh Fermor arrived the *Regnum Marianum* votive chapel was built near Városliget—the great city park. In 1951, the church was blown up on the orders of Communist dictator Mátyás

Rákosi in his anxious but unsuccessful drive to ban religion. The church was replaced with an enormous statue of Stalin, which was partly smelted from bronze taken from the equestrian statue of Count Gyula Andrássy, one of the architects of the Compromise of 1867, which established the Dual Monarchy. Stalin's statue was one of the first symbolic victims of the 1956 Revolution. By a curious twist of fate, bronze from the Stalin statue has recently been used to put a replacement equestrian statue of Count Andrássy in its original location on the banks of the Danube, near parliament and almost directly opposite Leigh Fermor's billet in Buda. Speaking at the launch party, Andrássy's descendant, Prince Mark Odescalchi, told his audience the melting down of the statue of his distinguished ancestor was analogous to what happened to his own family under the Nazis and during Communism. We will encounter many of these people and their fate later on in the Leigh Fermor story.

Soon after arriving in Buda the young English traveller began to realize this part of the Hungarian capital was talismanic territory for the Hungarians. So much of their history found an emblematic resonance in this medieval part of the city. He soon began to get his bearings in the ancient quarter and was taking note of how the streets 'sank like trenches between silent walls'. Within a decade of Leigh Fermor's arrival, this historic place would face near obliteration. The *Vár* became one of the sites of the Axis' last stand during the Siege of Budapest in 1945 and paid a heavy price for the role.

When Leigh Fermor arrived in 1934 the *Vár* still contained the residential palaces, or *palota* in Hungarian, of the old noble and gentry families. In truth, many of these locally aggrandized buildings were two-storey townhouses, though some were fine examples of more recent Hungarian monarchy and much earlier architectural styles.

PLF's bedroom 15 Úri utca 1934

Many of them contained all the splendid and often over-blown decorative elements characteristic of those styles of architecture. Some were indeed of very stately proportion. In these houses, as Sándor Márai observes of his own less grand family home in Buda, 'the tastes and habits of our ancestors had selected everything arranged in our rooms'. Or perhaps put less subtly, a gentleman in those days never bought his own furniture.

Aristocratic and wealthy merchant families built their townhouses in Úri utca as early as the thirteenth century when King Béla IV built the first royal residence in Buda. They wished, among other considerations, to be close to the seat of power and centre of defence offered by the castle. The destruction wrought by the war with the Turks occasioned the need to build new houses and many of these were in the baroque and neoclassical styles. These are the houses which greeted Leigh Fermor's attentive eye as he arrived in the *Vár*. The earliest structures can still be seen today in the part north of the intersection with Szentháromság utca or Holy Trinity Street. There was much at his doorstep to whet Leigh Fermor's avid appetite for historical detail. Field Marshal András Hadik (1710–1790), whose equestrian statue guards the crossing at Úri utca and Szentháromság utca, had been resident at number 58. He received preferment under Empress Maria Theresa after his considerable military achievements, including temporary victory over Berlin during the Seven Years' War. The observant visitor will note the highly polished bronze testicles of the Field Marshal's mount. This is the result of years of fervent rubbing by Hungarian students anxious to invoke good luck prior to sitting for examinations; a charming residuum of local voodoo. Number 53 Úri utca had once been a Franciscan Monastery but was sequestered for use as a residence for Emperor Joseph II in 1789. Just around the corner at Bécsikapu tér (Vienna Gate Square), number 7 played host to Thomas Mann as he fled Nazi Germany and arrived in Budapest just a few months after Leigh Fermor's departure. Incidentally, it was

Field Marshal András Hadik's statue in the *Vár* (c. 1930) near the house where PLF stayed in Buda

a man now considered to be a pariah by some and a reha-
bilitated scholarly saint by others, Bálint Hóman, who was
involved in organizing Mann's visa for Hungary.

Leigh Fermor's invitation to stay with the von Bergs came
by way of a letter of introduction from Tibor von Thuroczy de Alsóköröskény whose wife had given him the letter
of introduction for the Mayor of Esztergom. Leigh Fermor
made his acquaintance among the many people he had encountered in Bratislava. Von Thuroczy was friendly with at
least half a dozen of the Hungarian families to whom Leigh
Fermor received letters of introduction. He was also the
brother-in-law of Baron Fülöp 'Pips' von Schey de Koromla, incidentally—the brother of Edmund de Waal's great-
grandmother, Emmy Schey von Koromla. In de Waal's *The
Hare with Amber Eyes* there is a very engaging account of
Leigh Fermor's host Pips von Schey and life at his estate
where he was a guest. The Baron had become something of
a father figure to him on the earlier leg of his journey, before his crossing into Hungary. He saw him as something
of a Proustian reincarnation, half patrician, half scholar,
and even then he felt 'threatened with extinction'. He stayed
with him at his estate in Kövecsespuszta, today Štrkovec,
in Slovakia, about forty kilometres north-east of Bratislava.
The house is now a home for the disabled.

In 1858 a Jewish ancestor and namesake of his was granted an Austrian patent of nobility and was created a Baron.
The patent mentions it was granted for services rendered
during the 1848 Revolution, something that can hardly have
endeared him to the Hungarians. As early as the thirteenth
century Hungarian kings had granted patents of nobility
to Jewish courtiers for services to the Crown. The Holy Roman Emperor ennobled the Jewish Ricci family in the sixteenth century. The ennoblement of Jews in the Empire be-

Engraving of Baron von Schey's house at Kövecsespuszta, today Štrkovec in Slovakia

tween 1701 and 1918 made up 4.3 per cent of all Austrian ennoblements and this ratio was quite near in number to the percentage of Jews in the monarchy. Franz Joseph ennobled over 120 Hungarian Jews in the later part of the nineteenth century, creating twenty-eight barons but not a single count. Later, towards the end of his reign when he needed money for the war effort, the Emperor scattered titles about like snuff at a wake. Jakob Wassermann, a German-born novelist of Jewish descent, resident in Vienna in the early part of the twentieth century, observed how Vienna's nobility had ceased to be the bulwark of society they once were and how the role fell to the new bourgeois class and to the ennobled Jews. Incidentally, Wassermann used the figure of Leigh Fermor's mentor Pips von Schey as a character in one of his novels. The von Schey family retained their Jewish faith and made generous bequests to the synagogue in Kőszeg, their former Hungarian home town. During World War II, the Jews of Kőszeg were among the last to be deported to Auschwitz in the summer of 1944.

Like so many of the aristocratic men with whom Leigh Fermor bonded on his journey, Pips von Schey had a military background. In 1915 he served as an Imperial liaison officer with the German high command in Berlin, where he was influential in securing a desk job for the poet Rainer Maria Rilke far away from the dangers of the front line. For Leigh Fermor, von Schey held a special position in his progress towards manhood. 'Being told by someone much older to stop calling him Sir may have had something to do with it. It was a sort of informal investiture with the *toga virilis*.' Von Schey was fifty-three when Leigh Fermor befriended him.

If there were men on his journey who treated him as a mature young man, there were also many women who did the same. Among them was his Budapest hostess Baroness Erzsébet Gizella Eszter Mária von Berg, known as Berta.

Baroness Berta von Berg in the early 1930s

She was a plain-looking woman of about thirty-five when she played hostess to Leigh Fermor in Budapest. The later recollection of his youthful eye mistakenly placed her 'in her mid-forties' when he came to recall her in *Between the Woods and the Water*. She appears, from his account of her, to have been unpretentious and forthright. Her excellent English made her the ideal guide for the young Englishman during his first encounters with Budapest society. Her stepmother, the second wife of Count Sándor Nákó de Nagyszentmiklós, Hildegarde Maria Peters, had English blood, and as a girl Berta had visited England. Her father prospered under the Habsburgs and was appointed to the Privy Council. He was also a member of the upper house of the Hungarian parliament and was governor, during the time of the Hungarian suzerainty, of the much-disputed port of Fiume, today the Croatian port city of Rijeka. It served for many years as the Kingdom of Hungary's largest and most important port. By the time Count Nákó's daughter, Berta, married Tibor von Berg, the old count's financial circumstances had changed somewhat for the worse. A taste for high living had put a serious dent in the family fortune. By the time Tibor married Berta von Nákó there was very little by way of a dowry to add kindling to the fire of romance. Indeed, there appears to have been little there by way of true romance to begin with, according to Gloria von Berg. Tibor had been in love with a girl called Daisy Gray, whom he had met in London during his years there as a merchant banker. This love match was not encouraged by Tibor's father because Daisy was a 'Gaiety Girl'—one of those Edwardian beauties who entertained in music hall comedies. Several of these girls married into the nobility, the best known being Rosie Boote, who married the fourth Marquess of Headfort in 1901 and was a great success in the role of Marchioness. Aware that he could not bring Daisy back to Budapest, he took her instead to Cairo and while there she conceived a daughter, whom Tibor would not see until an accident of fate on a beach in Bermuda in 1965 reunited father and daughter. With mounting parental pressure, coupled with the call of duty to serve his country, Tibor returned to Budapest as war loomed and married Berta.

Berta von Berg was a down-to-earth, no nonsense sort of woman. She dressed in the very English bluestocking mode of the day consisting of tweed jacket and heavy tweed skirt. Though the house on Úri utca was called a *'palais'* or *'palolu'* in Hungarian, she quickly informed Leigh Fermor. 'All rot, of course. We seem to have a passion for grand styles in Hungary. It's a perfectly ordinary townhouse.'

Today the house is, for the most part, back in the hands of Gloria von Berg, who occupies part of it. Part is still occupied by the descendant of a resident imposed during Communist times, another part by an Odescalchi Prince. During Leigh Fermor's time in Budapest the family, strapped for cash like so many post-Trianon Hungarian aristocrats, also rented out rooms. The chair 'embroidered with a blue rampant lion with a forked tail and a scarlet tongue' on which Leigh Fermor's borrowed dinner jacket was strewn, survived the ravages of war, German, Soviet and local plundering during Communist times, but little else remains of the original interior furnishings. Today the chair from Leigh Fermor's bedroom survives in proud talismanic proclamation of the will of the former 'enemy class' to have survived into modern times.

Berta von Berg's description of the building is accurate. It is a plain-fronted house consisting of a five-bay façade behind which stand solid rooms with vaulted ceilings. The ground floor rooms run off a central entrance hallway. This

The house at 15 Úri utca, much as it was when Leigh Fermor stayed there in 1934.
His bedroom window is at the bottom left

leads to a staircase on the left and further on there is a door-
way to a paved courtyard. The interior of the house today is
again physically much as it must have looked during Leigh
Fermor's stay, despite the best efforts of its former occupants, during the days of the People's Republic, to enforce,
as Gloria von Berg put it, 'the first rule of Communism—
let's make everything as ugly as possible'. The von Bergs
were evicted from the house in 1951 and given just an hour
to pack one small suitcase each. They were sent to internal
deportation to Kék a village in the far north-east of Hungary where they lived with a poor farming family. After taking part in the 1956 uprising Tibor and his second wife The-
odóra von Hegedűs emigrated to the United States. Tibor
died in 1987. An elderly aunt insisted on staying on and she
was given one room. She was later the victim of frequent
physical abuse from the new Communist tenants. They also
smashed up the magnificent eighteenth-century wood-burn-
ing stoves, ripped up the star-patterned parquet and used
the fine library bookcases for firewood and for storing potatoes. It was still decorated, in 1934, in what was called in

Hungary 'the English style', coupled with the local taste for good quality Biedermeier furniture. There was a fad among many of the Hungarian aristocracy for the 'English style' in house decoration and personal dress. Budapest tailors were frequently asked to copy the bespoke Savile Row cut. English dress codes were strictly adhered to. A gentleman never wore tweed or brown shoes in the city. English foxhounds were also very popular with Hungarian hunting squires and the descendants of these animals can still be seen in Hungary today. 'Gossip, cigar-smoke and Anglophilia floated in the air,' is how Leigh Fermor writes of this Hungarian disposition for all things English. But the basis for Hungarian Anglophilia had more solid roots than in the mere frippery of fashion trends and interior decoration. Hungarian interest in British eighteenth- and nineteenth-century intellectual theories was connected to the struggle for political and intellectual freedom at this time. Major figures among the Hungarian intelligentsia were ardent followers of David Hume. Ferenc Kazinczy, the leading figure of the Hungarian enlightenment, read Hume's *History of England* while incarcerated for his liberal nationalist ideas in the prison of Kufstein. Language was Kazinczy's first love and he is credited with the standardization of the Magyar tongue.

Just two years before Leigh Fermor arrived in Budapest, thirty schools in the city had the English language as a compulsory subject on the curriculum. Some Hungarian aristocratic families sent their children to be schooled in England. Leigh Fermor mentions a young Hungarian aristocrat and poet, Ferenc Békássy, in *Between the Woods and the Water*. He and his five siblings were all sent from their home in Zsennye in western Hungary to Bedales School in Hampshire. Békássy went on to King's College, Cambridge, where he befriended people like John Maynard Keynes and Rupert Brooke and was elected to membership of the Apostles. He died fighting with the Hungarian army on the Eastern Front on June 25, 1915. A month before his death he wrote to an English girlfriend: 'By the time I go, there will be roses and I shall go with a crest of three red ones on my horse's head (but people won't know the reason) because there are three over the shield in our coat-of-arms. This isn't at all the letter I meant to write, but I can't help it. I long to see you. [...] And we shall meet again, shan't we, one day?' Leigh Fermor kept up a correspondence with the poet's sister Éva in later years. As a 'woman of action' she appealed to him. She had taken flying lessons from László Almásy, 'the English patient', and was one of the first women in Hungary to take to the wheel of a car. She married for the third time at the age of eighty. Eva made many trips to Greece where she sometimes met Leigh Fermor, thus connecting him again with the vanished world of old aristocratic Hungary. She died in Vienna in 1997 at the age of ninety-nine.

Éva Békássy at the wheel of her car in Hungary in 1925

Interior 15 Úri utca 1934

Though the fashion for all things English was widely recognized in Hungary, there were some of a contrarian disposition, especially among the Budapest intelligentsia, who were of the opinion the Hungarian upper classes simply mimicked *la mode anglaise* without knowing quite what they were doing. One who took such a view was the poet and francophile György Faludy, who in his memoir *My Happy Days in Hell*, outlines the opinion representative of some among Budapest's literary set. 'The lowest class of the West-lovers consisted of the dandies and the old gentlemen dressed in cloth from Manchester who sat at small tables of the Danube cafés, reading *The Times* even if, as it sometimes happened, they understood not a word of it. *The Times* was their letter-patent of nobility.' This is a rather cynical view of the genuine affection felt for England by many among the Hungarian aristocracy at this time. Great friendships were struck up between members of the English and Hungarian nobility. Tom Mitford, son of Lord Redesdale and only brother to all those Mitford sisters, used to stay with Countess Hanna

The poet Ferenc Békássy

Mikes at her family estate at Zabola (Zăbala) in Transylvania's Szeklerland. She was then married to her first husband, Count Géza Teleki de Szék, members of whose family Leigh Fermor had encountered in Budapest and would encounter again further along in his journey. He writes passionately of the Székelyföld or Szeklerland, an ethnographic region lost to Hungary in 1920 and briefly regained under the Second Vienna award in 1940 as a reward for Hungary's support for Germany in World War II. The area is infused with an almost sacerdotal presence in the mind of many Hungarians because the Szeklers were the sacred defenders of Hungary's ancient borders. Even today the Szekler flag flies alongside the Hungarian flag over the great entrance doors of the parliament building in Budapest and the region's anthem, the 'Székely himnusz', brings tears to the eyes of many a burly Hungarian as it expresses Hungary's desire to be united with this ancient land, ending in the aspirational refrain, 'Don't let Transylvania be lost to us, our God!'

As well as conventional friendships, there was at least one unconventional sexual relationship between a member of Hungary's old order and a flighty and rather unhinged member of the English upper-class. Unity Mitford, the Nazi-obsessed daughter of Lord Redesdale, was a regular visitor to Hungary in the 1930s. Her middle name 'Valkyrie' coupled with her extreme right-wing, anti-Semitic views, and the fact she was conceived in the Canadian mining town of Swastika, Ontario, where her family had interests in gold mines, made her extremely attractive to Hitler, who set great store by such absurd omens. The Führer would also have been aware of her relationship to Winston Church ill. She befriended Hitler in Munich. In later years Leigh Fermor became a close friend of her sister Deborah Mitford, Duchess of Devonshire. Unity Mitford's social connections in Budapest included people later persecuted by her Nazi friends. Amongst those who entertained her were Count Imre and Countess Marie-Eugenie Zichy, the Duke and Duchess of Mecklenburg and Countess 'Baby' Erdődy— whose family would later flee from the Nazis. The Duke of Mecklenburg was arrested by the Gestapo and sent to Sachsenhausen concentration camp. Miss Mitford's introduction to Hungary came through her friendship and rather outré sexual relationship with János von Almásy, a bisexual and brother of 'the English patient', László Ede Almásy. Like his brother, his sexual tastes were varied to say the least. Miss Mitford's sexual antics were said to run to servicing members of a favoured group of Storm Troopers. The bisexual Almásy had an obsessive interest in the occult and in horoscopes. He had briefly been the lover of Unity's brother, Tom Mitford, but Almásy also became her partner in what she once described to Baroness Gaby Bentinck (Hinie Thyssen's sister) as 'savage fornication'. By her own account this involved near asphyxiation at some point in the kinky proceedings. It was Almásy, a confirmed Nazi supporter, who retrieved Unity's personal papers after her unsuccessful attempt to commit suicide in Munich in 1939 following England's declaration of war on Germany. No doubt his haste to do so was partly motivated by what he might find contained therein about himself. While staying

János Almásy (left), Unity Mitford (second left), and Almásy's wife Marie (née Princess Esterházy) in the 1930s

at Bernstein, the Almásy estate in Burgenland, Unity Mitford once threatened to report her host to Hitler when his estate manager, who was Jewish, offered to bring the house party to a service in a local synagogue. Further along in his journey Leigh Fermor would meet more conventional and somewhat more charming members of the comital branch of the Almásy family.

Five years before Leigh Fermor's arrival in Budapest, a grateful city erected a fountain to mark an English aristocrat's devotion to the nation. Lord Rothermere's unconditional support for Hungary in the wake of the disastrous Treaty of Trianon was much appreciated in Budapest. Rothermere lost two sons in the Great War but was moved to say in Hungary's defence: 'They sacrificed their lives for noble ideas but not so which people would do so unjustly with a glorious nation. There won't be peace in Europe until the cunning and insensible Treaty of Trianon is revised.'

Count Albert Apponyi (left) with Count Mihály Károlyi

The treaty, signed in 1920, reduced the kingdom's territories by two-thirds; reduced its population by 64 per cent and left millions of ethnic Hungarians stranded outside the new borders of the motherland. It also deprived Hungary of its access to the sea. It fell to Count Albert Apponyi to do his best to defend Hungary's interests during what can hardly be called the Treaty negotiations but rather the ultimatum presented to Hungary. Apponyi's speech was one of the legendary pieces of oratory presented at Versailles and is described thus by a Scandinavian journalist at the time: 'Apponyi talked with such rhetorical master-strokes, so lightly, elaborately and precisely in his two hour long speech in English, French and Italian which no one has ever done before in the world, which no parliament has ever heard. He defended his homeland with such touching words which many delegates couldn't mask their emotions.'

Of everything which was taken from Hungary at Trianon, no loss was comparable to that of Transylvania. Not even the Turkish occupation for 158 years carries with it such a deep-rooted and bitter memory in the Hungarian national consciousness as the consequences of Trianon. Winston Churchill told the House of Commons: 'Those who are not to reconsider the prejudice of Trianon are preparing a new European war.' A view shared by Neville Chamberlain who added: 'The result of the Treaty of Trianon in Europe is not peace, but the fear of another war.'

Lord Rothermere stoutly advocated revision of the treaty in Hungary's favour. In June 1927 he used his own newspaper, the *Daily Mail*, to publish a detailed plan for restoration to Hungary of large tracts of the territory it had lost as a direct result of the treaty. This pro-Hungarian stance made him something of a hero in Hungary. His detractors in England, however, were ambiguous about his impassioned defence of the Hungarian cause. Rumours were circulating in London that the press baron had been won over to Hungary's defence by the sexual enticements of a Hungarian temptress. She was actually the Austrian Princess Stephanie von Hohenlohe, the daughter of a Viennese Jewish dentist who had married into the Austro-Hungarian nobility and had wormed her way into influential circles in London society. She was a known German spy in London during the 1930s. In 1933, when Hitler became Chancellor, MI6 confirmed that the French secret service had uncovered documents during a search of the princess's Paris flat which in-

Rothermere fountain, Budapest

structed her to use her female charms on Rothermere to get his support for the return to Germany of lands ceded to Poland at the end of the Great War. She was in the pay of both the Germans and of Rothermere. Rumours even circulated that Rothermere had an interest in being placed on the Hungarian throne, which, given Admiral Horthy's resistance to placing the crowned and anointed King back on the throne was preposterous. The memorial fountain to Rothermere in Budapest survived Communism and still stands near the former Wenckheim Palace (now the Szabó Ervin Library), on the corner of Reviczky utca and Ötpacsirta utca.

Back at 15 Úri utca, the entrance hall contains a telling memorial to the role the house played during World War II. A support beam bears a colourful enamelled plaque telling the visitor the house 'is under the protection of the Swedish Crown'. The house was used by Swedish diplomat Raoul

15 Úri utca, sign indicates protection under the Crown of Sweden

Wallenberg as one of his 'safe houses' in Budapest for the purpose of hiding Jewish families. Beneath the house runs a warren of underground passages which must have proven most useful to Wallenberg in his brave task. It was also in this subterranean maze Wallenberg kept his stockpile of cash for emergency use in feeding Jewish families, providing the all-important *Schutzpass* and bringing people back from the forced death marches. The house was given over to Wallenberg for several weeks during the height of the final push to round up Budapest's Jews. The von Berg family had been involved with Wallenberg since his arrival in Budapest in July 1944 through the activities of Berta von Berg's aunt, Countess Erzsébet Nákó. She was fervently anti-Fascist and worked closely with Wallenberg in the rescue of some of the many Jews he saved. She was also in love with Wallenberg, but it was unrequited.

It was from this hospitable house Leigh Fermor was taken on a twelve-day social spree which gave him further connections to some of the people who passed him on to their aristocratic friends. These were people whose country houses were dotted along his route as he made his way through the Great Hungarian Plain, the Banat and Transylvania and progressed in the direction of Constantinople. In Budapest he collected his monthly allowance from the local British Legation, a habit formed since he first set out on his journey. While collecting his allowance in Budapest he made the acquaintance of William Evelyn Houstoun-Boswall, the British number two at the Legation. Houstoun-Boswall had fought with distinction in the First World War

Raoul Wallenberg in Budapest.

and was awarded a Military Cross, again conforming to the type that Leigh Fermor so admired when a young man. So hospitable were his Hungarian hosts that he found it almost impossible to pay for anything. Neither did they care about his often dishevelled appearance. 'Tigers for turnout, they were well-groomed in what used to be thought the English style; but they didn't give a damn about my rough-and-ready outfit. The best I could manage was a tweed coat and some grey canvas trousers, which, with a clean shirt and a blue tie, looked almost presentable; but the footgear

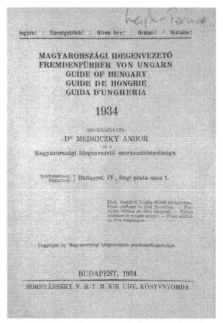

PLF's own copy of Guide to Hungary 1934.

let me down—this was always gym or tennis shoes, which-ever looked cleaner. But it didn't matter.' What may have mattered, at least slightly, that he was an extremely sloven-ly house guest, with scant regard for the normal conven-tions usually involved in staying with other people. Mon-ogrammed bed sheets were further adorned with cigarette burns. Ancient oriental carpets were given additional pat-ination by overturned coffee cups. But he was right. None of this mattered and the majority of his hosts wanted him to stay on for longer than he intended.

Some commentators on his writing about this period have remarked on the fact he completely ignored the stir-ring political times in which he travelled. 'Why did Patrick Leigh Fermor fail to see the wind of political change which was blowing around him in Budapest and elsewhere on his journey in the wake of Hitler's accession to the chancellorship?' is the question which is still sometimes asked. Others of his age, class and generation were ready witnesses to these extraordinary political times. The example is sometimes given of Auden and Isherwood, who were in Berlin in the late 1920s and were only slightly older than Leigh Fermor. They were acutely aware of the political changes happening around them. The simple answer, if there ever is such a thing, is very few even more seasoned observers among the Hungarians themselves were aware of the calamity coming their way. Even with the benefit of hindsight— *Between the Woods and the Water* was published in 1986— Leigh Fermor makes no mention of the guiding force then pushing Hungary towards an extreme right-wing, anti-Semitic position and into the arms of Hitler. That man was Gyula Gömbös, who succeeded Count Gyula Károlyi as Prime Minister in 1932. Gömbös had an intense dislike of

The coronation of Emperor Charles and Empress Zita as King and Queen of Hungary, Budapest 1916. Crown Prince Otto is in the centre of the picture

Prime Minister Gyula Gömbös, who boasted of an identical chest size
to that of Mussolini

the Jews, little time for the aristocracy and a lifetime detestation of the Habsburg monarchy. On November 13, 1918,
Charles IV had surrendered his powers as Hungarian monarch; however, he did not abdicate the throne thus making
Horthy's eventual regency possible but also introducing the
possibility of regaining the Crown of St Stephen. Gömbös
was a key organizer of one of the attempts by elements of
the Hungarian army, and a group of enthusiastic students,
to prevent the by then very unlikely restoration of Charles
to the throne of Hungary in 1921. The resulting so-called
Battle of Budaörs, named after an area to the west of the
capital where the encounter took place, was no more than a
minor disorganized armed skirmish between royalists and
their opponents. It finally put an end to Charles's claim to
the Hungarian throne. It also, in a way, laid a marker for the
radical right's ascendancy in Hungarian political life, which
survived with imperceptible intrusions until 1945.

Gömbös wanted a middle-class hegemony firmly rooted in Christian conservative values. As if to publicly affirm

his extreme right-wing credentials, his first visit as Prime Minister outside of the country was to Mussolini. His second foreign visit was to Hitler. Gömbös became the first head of a foreign sovereign nation to make a private visit to the Nazi leader. His detestation of all things aristocratic did not prevent him accepting so many orders and decorations that when dressed up in full kit his uniform barely had enough chest room to contain all the gongs. Rather oddly, he frequently boasted to intimates his chest measurement was identical to that of Mussolini's.

There were few in Budapest in 1934 who predicted what the future political landscape would look like. One who *did* was Miksa Fenyő. His was a rare early voice raised in accurate warning against the potential dangers for Hungary of the steady rise of Hitler and Nazism. He was a member of parliament and co-founder of the influential literary magazine *Nyugat* (West). He published a pamphlet in 1934 called *Hitler: Egy Tanulmány* (*Hitler: A Study*) in which he made quite clear his views on the threat posed by Hitler to Hungary and to the European order. He was later one of the first Hungarians to be placed on a death list by Hitler. After the war, Stalin wanted him sent to Siberia, a fate he escaped by fleeing Hungary. His was an intelligent voice frequently raised in protest and just as frequently ignored. He had written brilliantly on the consequences of the Treaty of Trianon for Hungary. He was an eloquent and clever orator in parliament. He was a Jew who converted to Catholicism but was at heart an agnostic.

Leigh Fermor has a brief reference to Hitler and to the 'Night of the Long Knives' or *Röhm-Putsch* in *Between the Woods and the Water*, but it applies to events during the later Transylvanian leg of his journey: '[S]tartling news from outside had reached our valley. In the middle of the night, Hitler, Goering and Himmler had rounded up and murdered many of their colleagues, and a number—perhaps several hundred—of the rank and file of the SA. Nobody knew how to interpret these bloody portents but they spread dismay and little else was spoken of for a day or two; and then the topic died, drowned by the heat and the weight of summer.'

He also mentions his transitory interest in politics in his letter to Xan Fielding in the introductory section of the book: 'News of grim events kept breaking in from the outside world but something in the mood of these valleys and mountain ranges weakened their impact. They were omens, and sinister ones, but there were three more years to go before these omens pointed unmistakably to the convulsions five years later.'

One can hardly expect a nineteen-year-old, even one with an exceptional interest in history, to be aware of, or indeed keenly interested in, the subtleties of political life in the Hungarian capital in the complex times of the Regent Horthy. It would also be unhelpful to think of him then as the more seasoned political observer he became in later years, especially on Greek politics, and perhaps invidious also to invite comparisons with people of Auden's intellectual stature. The fact the book was written long after the period in which he travelled through Hungary certainly provided an opportunity to enlighten his readers more on the contemporary political atmosphere of 1934 Hungary and to dwell less on the minutiae of ancient history. A review of the book in the *New York Times* refers to 'distant lightning from events in Germany weirdly illuminates the trail of this free spirit'. It is very distant indeed, apart from 'the crunch of measured footfalls' of Stormtroopers making their presence felt in far-off towns before he reached the Hungarian border. But he does not labour the point nor does he develop it with the benefit of hindsight. That he chose not to add such embellishment later is greatly to his credit. Jan Morris, in her introduction to the 2005 edition of *Between the Woods and the Water*, comments on his lack of interest and also the apparent lack of interest among his hosts in contemporary politics: 'He seems to have had no sense of it at the time. He was not much interested in politics. Hitler had come to power in 1933 but Leigh Fermor took little notice as he hiked through Germany. When he heard that the Austrian Chancellor Dr Dollfuss had been assassinated and yet another ominous step towards catastrophe taken, "the gloom didn't last much longer than breakfast." Few yet knew the full impact of it. Leigh Fermor, as he said himself, didn't give a damn and as he proceeded through Hungary to Rumania, his several hosts, whether sporting or scholarly, seldom seemed to have raised contemporary political issues. They were obsessed with their pasts, and perhaps preferred not to dwell upon their futures', is how he recalled them.

In *Between the Woods and the Water*, he does recall a fleeting encounter he had with a group of Orthodox Jews in the Carpathian Mountains with whom he talks about Hitler's rise to power and the issue of Nazi Germany is discussed as though it might just be something transitory: 'They came into the conversation and—it seems utterly incredible now— we talked of Hitler and the Nazis as though they merely represented a dire phase of history, a sort of transitory aberration or a nightmare that might suddenly vanish, like a cloud evaporating or a bad dream.'

He did record several meetings he had with one of the most interesting and controversial of Hungary's contemporary political figures, Count Pál Teleki de Szék, but again rather surprisingly expresses little interest in the extraordinary role this man had played in modern political life

Count Pál Teleki who befriended PLF in Budapest

in Hungary. Teleki was born in Budapest on November 1, 1879. and belonged to the old aristocratic order. He was a man of essentially academic disposition who, like so many of his class felt duty bound to enter political life. He had studied political science and geography at the University of Budapest, receiving his doctoral degree in 1903. That year he made an extensive geographical expedition to the Sudan. He had been Foreign Minister three times in separate administrations and was a former, and, when Leigh Fermor met him, future Prime Minister. It was under his premiership the Treaty of Trianon was ratified by the Hungarian parliament in 1920. He was later prompted by Hungary's ill-advised support for Hitler and by his own prevarication over that support, to commit suicide in 1941. Hungary had signed a nonaggression pact with Yugoslavia in December 1940 and when it reneged on the agreement and facilitated the German invasion of Yugoslav territories in April 1941 Teleki shot himself.

In the early days of his stay in Budapest, Leigh Fermor was a guest at 7 József Nádor tér, a house which had been for many years the epicentre of Budapest's political and intellectual life. He was invited on a number of occasions. It was the imposing town palace of Count Pál Teleki and his family but presided over in those days by the formidable figure of his mother, the Dowager Countess Teleki de Szék (née Irén Muráty). She was from the exceptionally wealthy Muráty family of Greek merchants who had invested heavily in Budapest real estate and accumulated a large fortune. In the 1880s in addition to the house on József Nádor tér they had properties in the fifth, sixth and seventh districts of the city. As many as 10,000 Greeks migrated to Hungary in the eighteenth century. By the nineteenth century the Muráty family was already rich from extensive trading interests in Trieste and their Budapest property holdings.

It was this formidable woman who further raised her family's profile by marrying into one of the grandest Hungarian families. By 1934 she controlled not only the purse strings but also the manner in which the household operated. When the crusty old Dowager placed her knife and fork in the customary position to indicate one has finished eating, the entire table, whether finished eating or not, was expected to follow suit. Not to do so would have been to embrace a form of social death in the Budapest of those days.

One can only imagine the sense of surprise this *grande dame* had when Leigh Fermor casually ambled in late for lunch, dressed in a manner which must have caused the old dowager some unease. However, as was to be the story for the remainder of his time in Hungary and elsewhere, his charm, intelligence, boyish enthusiasm and good looks won

PLF much as he looked in Budapest in 1934

over the day. The Telekis, one of the most influential families in Hungary, were captivated by this young man who had undertaken a journey the very idea of which fascinated them.

It is not surprising that Pál Teleki took a special interest in the young adventurer. He was a distinguished geographer who had mapped the Japanese archipelago and helped draw up the frontiers of Mesopotamia. He was head of the Hungarian Scout Movement and a friend of the English scouting legend Lord Baden-Powell. There is a charming story of how Teleki became interested in scouting. His son Géza was on a visit to Denmark with the Hungarian Sea Scouts in 1927—a relic of the days of Empire when Hungary still had access to the sea. When he proved negligent in some minor nautical task the team leader said he would report him to his father on their return to Budapest. Young Teleki retorted he could go ahead and do so because his father had absolutely no interest in scouting. When this was reported back to Count Teleki he resolved there and then to become completely immersed in scouting. Géza Teleki, a reluctant sea scout, went on to represent Hungary in hockey at the Berlin Olympic Games in Berlin in 1936. Géza was just four years older than Leigh Fermor but sadly they do not appear to have met, or if they did he does not record the meeting. They did correspond in later years.

It was not unusual for Leigh Fermor to eschew the company of his own age group for that of older people. He returned to the Teleki palace on other occasions during his twelve-day stay in Budapest to pour over maps and books and listen to the stories from the then fifty-five-year-old Count. In *Between the Woods and the Water*, he leaves us a charming portrait of this tragic figure: '[A]cross the table, he told us stories of travel among the Turks and the Arabs when he was helping to draw the frontiers of Mesopotamia. He broke off for lively descriptions of Abdel Hamid and Slatin Pasha, that strange Anglo-Austrian for years the running-footman of the Mahdi. The Count's alert, pointed face behind horn-rimmed spectacles, lit by a quick, witty and enthusiastic manner, had an almost Chinese look. It is hard to think of anyone kinder.'

The Teleki/Muráty Palace at 7 József Nádor tér in the 1930s
(today the Bank of China)

There were, and still are, some in Hungary who do not consider Pál Teleki in such a kind light. It was under his premiership that the first anti-Jewish law, the *Numerus Clausus*, was introduced in Hungary in 1920. Though the actual legislation did not use the exact term 'Jew', an executive order drawn up after the legislation was promulgated specifically mentions the Jews as a separate race. Its aim was specifically geared at limiting what was seen by many Hungarians as the over-representation of Jews in higher education and consequently certain professions such as law and medicine. Teleki was an old-fashioned Hungarian aristocratic nationalist and had no specific personal hatred of the Jews. He saw it in terms of demographics and immigration in the post-Trianon period, as he explained in a series of lectures given at the Institute of Politics in Williamstown, Massachusetts, during the summer of 1921. It represents the views held by many of Leigh Fermor's aristocratic hosts and is one of the few contemporary statements made by a Hungarian politician abroad on the subject.

'I should like to say that it is a mistake to think that the anti-Jewish movement, which really existed and which still exists in Hungary, is one against the Jewish religion or Jews in general. If I had to characterize it as a historian it would be rather with the words "anti-Galician movement". It is much more a question of immigration, and antagonism towards a certain group of foreigners who turned against the nation.' He went on to characterize Hungarian anti-Semitism as stemming from Hungary's liberal immigration policy and offered the argument popular at the time of Jewish involvement in the Communist administration of Béla Kun.

In 1785 we had 75,000 Jews in Hungary, who were on the best of terms with the Magyars and with the other peoples, and who began very strongly to amalgamate and fuse with the Magyars and other races. In 1910 we had 912,000 Jews, not counting those who were Christianized, who would amount to a few hundred thousand. You see the volume of immigration must have been very large because between these figures of 75,000 and 912,000 there lies only a century. It was at its height towards the close of the period in question, and was a consequence of persecution of Jews in Roumania and Russia, and of liberalism in Hungary. This produced a great influx of Jewish population from these two countries into Hungary. The great danger was not that there were many men of Jewish religion in Hungary—not at all. The danger was that we had a large immigration of foreigners, who by our very liberal laws were too soon made citizens and given the same rights as old citizens before they had any feeling of loyalty for the land and for their fellow-countrymen. Practically they were allowed to acquire citizenship in one and all political rights in five years. We recognized all our dangers of immigration too late. You are recognizing dangers inherent to immigration in time; and we may blame ourselves for not having done so. Bolshevism in Hungary was led and directed by these foreigners. Of course, there were Jews of older Hungarian origin, just as there were Hungarians taking part in the bolshevist movement, but the hatred of the people was aroused by the Galicians.

This latter remark was typical of the selective anti-Semitism of some of the politicians of the period, including the Regent, Miklós Horthy, who drew a distinction between assimilated or Magyarized Jews and immigrants, especially those from 'Galicia'. The distinction would do little to save the many who were deported later.

An intemperate anti-Semitic speech Teleki made in the upper house was typical of the prevailing attitude among many politicians who used the threat of Nazi pressure to further legitimize anti-Jewish legislation. He counted some of the Hungarian Jewish intelligentsia among his friends but yet he was convinced of the need to restrict Jewish academic influence in Hungary. Teleki was an avowed anti-Nazi whose personal detestation of Hitler forced him into near complete silence when he met him in 1940. It would have been extremely difficult for him, coming from a family background like his, to have had anything but disdain for Hitler. The body language of photographs from his meeting with Hitler illustrates the point. Teleki is seen unsmiling and with clenched fists. It is all the more unfortunate, therefore, that he played into Hitler's hands and oversaw the introduction of further anti-Jewish legislation during his second period as Prime Minister between 1939 and 1941. In an attempt to counter the wave of anti-Semitic propaganda being published in Hungary at this time, a book called *Itéljetek!* (Judge!) appeared. Written by Márton Vida, it listed the many achievements in science, culture and sport of Magyarized Jews and it directly challenged the work of the black propagandists, such as the film *Jud Süß* (Süss the Jew, 1940), which portrayed Jews as greedy and unpatriotic.

Of the seven Prime Ministers who governed between 1938 and 1945 it was during Teleki's premiership that the largest number of statutes and decrees affecting Jews were promulgated. These were of mixed variety, mostly restricting Jewish membership of the professions, representation in the legislature and on municipal boards. It fell to the most anti-Semitic Prime Minister, and leader of the fascist Arrow Cross Party, Ferenc Szálasi, to introduce the most devastating piece of anti-Semitic legislation. It restricted Jew-

Teleki meeting Hitler in Vienna, 1940 (note Teleki's clinched fists)

ish wealth and essentially channelled it into the state's and into private coffers by registering and sequestering Jewish property and allowing a near free-for-all for those who wished to steal Jewish property and goods. Many Teleki supporters today stoutly defend his reputation and say it is unlikely that a civilized and cultured man like Teleki would have stood by and allowed the deportation of so many Hungarian Jews to the death camps. His distant kinswoman, the very pro-British Judith Lady Listowel, born Judith de Márffy-Mantuano, in Kaposvár in south-western Hungary, certainly did not believe Teleki to be anti-Semitic. On the declaration of war in 1939 Lady Listowel sought to convince both Count Ciano, Mussolini's son-in-law, and Teleki not to side with Hitler.

The number of Communists of Jewish background involved in the foundation of the Soviet Republic of 1919 is often cited as the reason for the rise of anti-Semitism in Hungary. István Pogany, a retired academic, in an as yet unpublished memoir about his Jewish family in Hungary argues that the average Hungarian Jewish citizen had as much dislike of the hard core Marxists as the next man. 'It's hardly surprising that the vast majority of Hungary's Jews loathed Marxism and revolution of any kind. Apart from considerations of religious faith—Communism's categorical rejection of religion was anathema to the observant—even most secular-minded Jews were deeply sceptical

Judith, Countess of Listowel, by Bassano

of Marxism and its utopian claims. The great majority of Hungary's Jews, whether shopkeepers, artisans, small businessmen, bookkeepers, doctors, teachers, bank clerks, veterinarians or engineers, believed that they had far more to lose than to gain from the triumph of Marxism-Leninism and the establishment of the dictatorship of the proletariat.'

Pogany clearly demonstrates in a dispassionate and factual way how the average Jewish citizen was as likely to be a victim of Soviet oppression as his Christian fellow citizen.

As early as April 1919, the Hungarian Soviet closed down all Jewish institutions, including the *Chevra Kadisha* or bereavement society. Jewish newspapers and magazines were banned, while the assets of religious denominations, both Jewish and Christian, were confiscated. Jewish as well as non-Jewish landowners, businessmen, industrialists and bankers were deprived of their property in sweeping measures of nationalization that even impacted on artisans and craftsmen, whose modest workshops were appropriated by the state. Jewish traders and shopkeepers, like their non-Jewish peers, were frequently branded as 'saboteurs' by the Soviet and blamed for shortages of food and other essentials that gave rise to growing anger and disillusionment amongst the general public.

Leigh Fermor did not refer to the perceived anti-Semitic side of Teleki's character even when publishing fifty years after first meeting him. For the most part he avoids the issue of anti-Semitism in Hungary. He does say, however, that his way of dealing with it was to try and steer clear of it whenever it arose as a topic of conversation with his aristocratic hosts. Anti-Semitism was the one area of common ground he found between some of his Hungarian and Rumanian hosts. He later wrote about being shown copies of the *Semi-Gotha* by a Hungarian aristocrat. The *Semi-Gotha* was published in 1912, 1913, and 1914 and formed a comprehensive account of those of Jewish ancestry who were now members of the titled European nobility. It was later used by the Nazis as a source of identification of Jewish families and individuals for transportation to the extermination camps. Quotations from its preface were sometimes used by anti-Semites as solid evidence that the Jews' eventual aim was world domination. 'Let us not forget where we came from! No more "German" Jews, no more "Portuguese" Jews! We are dispersed over the whole world, but still only one people!' declared Rabbi Salomon Lippmann. 'We are the chosen people! Proud may we keep our heads up and demand special right to be adored. We should not only have equal rights, but preferred rights!' said Dr Bernhard Cohn in 1899. He was also shown a copy of *The Protocols of the Elders of Zion*, a fabricated text first published in Russia in 1903 which claimed to be of Jewish authorship and was also offered as irrefutable proof by anti-Semites of the Jewish plan for world economic domination. It was certainly not of major interest to a young Englishman in Budapest wishing to have a good time. To someone like Leigh Fermor, who was intelligent but also had the ready affability of a 'hail-fellow-well-met' sort of young man, anti-Semitism was quite repulsive. However, when singing for one's supper even the righteous can sometimes find it difficult to be bold. He would already have been familiar with the anti-Semitism of the Bloomsbury set, part of which he had socialized with in London. Virginia Woolf, herself married to 'a penniless Jew' (as she referred to her husband Leonard), remarked about the aesthete and art collector Sir Philip Sassoon being 'an underbred Whitechapel Jew'. In the opinion of John Maynard Keynes, who was, like Leonard Woolf, a member of the Cambridge Apostles as well as a trenchant atheist, 'It is not agreeable to see civilisation so under the ugly thumbs of its impure Jews who have all the money and the power and brains.' It is unlikely Leigh Fermor heard any such talk in the Teleki household and if he did he was discreet enough not to record it.

Pál Teleki committed suicide in April 1941 when he felt it was the only honourable thing to do after what he saw as Hungary's betrayal of Yugoslavia. However there are some

Hungarians who still subscribe to the conspiracy theory that he may have been murdered. His son Géza Teleki went to Horthy and insisted on seeing all of the documentary evidence to show his father had committed suicide. It appears the Regent did not take well to what he considered as the insolence of the young man'. Horthy wrote to former Prime Minister Miklós Kállay in April 1947: 'so far as Géza Teleki is concerned, I have always thought that he was a man who was both restless and somewhat lacking in balance. He came up to see me after poor Boli's [Pál Teleki's] death and behaving in a totally inappropriate manner almost demanded that I show him his father's letter. This was a warm, touching letter of farewell in which he blamed himself needlessly. He could have read it but I was so upset by his impudent behaviour that I refused to let him have the letter. Perhaps it would have been better to have let him take a look at it and then throw him out. Now he probably thinks that he [Pál Teleki] blamed me for something.'

Among the evidence the young Teleki did not see was the suicide note which contained these chilling words: 'We broke our word,—out of cowardice. [...] The nation feels it, and we have thrown away its honour. We have allied ourselves to scoundrels. [...] We will become body snatchers! A nation of trash. I did not hold you back. I am guilty.' Winston Churchill was so upset at the news of Teleki's death he was moved to say: 'His suicide was a sacrifice to absolve himself and his people from guilt in the German attack on Yugoslavia. It clears his name before history.' Admiral Horthy wrote in his memoirs: 'With the death of Count Teleki, Hungary lost one of her foremost statesmen and I personally one of my most valued friends. It may well have been Count Teleki's tragedy that he was born too late. His sensitive, scholarly nature, his vast knowledge and his outstand-

The funeral cortege of Count Pál Teleki through Budapest

ing ability to foresee political developments would have enabled him to play a leading part at the Table of the 1878 Berlin Congress. He was not a man who could combat the ruthless totalitarian forces that were shaping the destinies of nations in his lifetime'.

If the coronation of King Charles IV had been one of the last great appearances in public of the Hungarian nobility *en masse*, then the funeral of Leigh Fermor's benefactor, Count Pál Teleki, on April 6, 1941, was truly the last such event in pre-Communist Budapest. Not since the funeral of Count Albert Apponyi, the defender of Hungary at Versailles, had their been such an outpouring of public grief. All the nobility were gathered wearing full regalia of egret-feathered and ermine-trimmed uniforms. Knights of St Stephen, Knights of the Order of the Golden Fleece, Knights of the Order of the Holy Sepulchre, Knights of Malta; all wearing orders and decorations which would soon be consigned to dusty attics, or looted by scavengers, were worn with great solemnity. Cardinal Serédi, whom Leigh Fermor saw in Esztergom, represented the Catholic Church. It was only marred for the family by the saluting of the coffin by an unwelcome delegation of Nazis carrying a wreath from Hitler and a delegation of Italian fascists carrying another from Mussolini. The horse-drawn hearse moved through the streets of Budapest bearing the hand-painted coat-of-arms of the Counts Teleki de Szék who were first granted their patent of nobility in the sixteenth century. The Regent, Admiral Horthy, was in the mourning party behind the hearse as the cortege moved in stately funereal progress through the streets of Budapest on its journey to Gödöllő, thirty kilometres north-east of Budapest. On that crisp spring day thousands paid their respects to the man who had played host to Patrick Leigh

The Regent Admiral Miklós Horthy de Nagybánya

Fermor a mere seven years earlier. Leigh Fermor himself would soon be part of a nation at war with a country he loved. Anglo-Hungarian relations were effectively buried with Pál Teleki. The day after his funeral the British recalled their minister to Budapest, the distinguished and quite pro-Hungarian Anglo-Irishman, Owen O'Malley. The legation building where Leigh Fermor had collected his monthly travel stipend closed soon after.

Leigh Fermor did not spend all of his time in scholarly pursuits in the private libraries of the capital. He had a growing and well-deserved reputation for sybaritic indulgence. This he had acquired among the upper-class bohemian fops in London with whom he had run after being expelled from the King's School, Canterbury. But before we track him to the fleshpots of Budapest it is worth noting to his credit that whenever a house he was staying in or visited had a decent library he never failed to notice and make use of it, often recording in his notebooks details of the volumes consulted.

The first thing he observed about the von Bergs' house was that 'there were books everywhere'. At the Teleki palace he found himself in a scholar's heaven. Pál Teleki was one of Budapest's greatest bibliophiles. It was said when times were financially tough he would make great sacrifices in order to purchase books. Indeed, contemporary visitors to the house noted the excellent library and the indifferent quality of the furniture for such a grand house. This bibliophile passion is easily understood when we consider his ancestor, Count Sámuel Teleki, founded in 1802 one of the greatest private libraries in Central Europe. It still operates according to its original charter today. His gift of 40,000 books for the Teleki Library in Marosvásárhely (Târgu Mureș) remains one of the most significant gifts made to Transylvania, of which Teleki was Chancellor. The library was nationalized during Communism and some of Teleki's descendants by then declared 'class enemies', survived by living in a tiny closet in the library. The space was so small one of them was forced to sleep on top of a cupboard. One member of the family, Countess Gemma Teleki, was permitted to live in a back corridor of the library and to eke out a miserable existence selling flowers and vegetables in the market square of Marosvásárhely (Târgu Mureș). She is still remembered in the city today. A member of the Samuel Teleki library staff recalled seeing her in the 1980s selling her home-grown produce. She recalled the wonder of a child in Communist times beholding a grand old lady in reduced circumstances: "we knew she was a Countess but we didn't quite know what a Countess was". Her former husband, also her cousin, Count Károly Teleki, known to his friends as 'Pufi' left Marosvásárhely (Târgu Mureș), taking with him from the library of which he was president, rare items to which he had no claim to ownership. These included the only Corvina, a Codex from one of the most extraordinary libraries of the Renaissance period, established by King Matthias Corvinus in the mid 15th century. He also took 14 incunabula, approximately 50 early Hungarian books and other extremely valuable and rare items which he sold to support his playboy existence in the South of France and elsewhere. The items disappeared in the 1920s and 1930s. To this day it has been impossible to re-acquire any of these books for the library or even, in the case of many of the lost items, to discover their present whereabouts.

Leigh Fermor would meet again with members of the Teleki family on the road to Constantinople but for now, in his remaining days in Budapest, his attention turned to fun and to romance.

Budapest never shared to the same degree in Berlin's reputation for sexual permissiveness or for raunchy nightlife. However, it was still a place were easy virtue was available for ready money. The women of Budapest were renowned for their beauty. They were so sought after by Eastern potentates that some, in the nineteenth century, even found their way to the *seraglios* of the Orient. In the mid-nineteenth century there were over forty licensed brothels in Budapest. The authorities regulated the activities of these houses of pleasure and monitored them from both the financial and health perspectives. At the end of the Great War the city lost one of its most legendary licentious establishments, The Black Cat, at 9 Király utca, a nightclub where sex was available with the hostesses for the exchange of a mere handful of *korona*. By the time Leigh Fermor arrived in Budapest, the conservative Horthy regime had clamped down on the operation of brothels in the city but not in a particularly heavy-handed way. Gone were the days of the grand *maison speciale*, like Mme Roza's at 20 Magyar utca, where even kings and princes were known to have taken their pleasure under the vigilant gaze of 'the Rose of Pest', as its Madam was known. In Slovakia, in the town of Nové Zámky, a musician he met in a cafe on hearing Leigh Fermor was headed for Budapest advised him to visit Maison Frieda 'where every man can be a "cavalier" for a mere five pengő' (the currency which replaced the korona in 1927). The 'Frieda Háza', as it was known locally, was still just about functioning at 29 Magyar utca when Leigh Fermor arrived in Budapest. This section of the 'Green Diary' is sadly blank, so neither history nor journal relate if he took the musician's advice and spent his pengős at this legendary pleasure dome. Incidentally, the pengő was Hungary's unit of currency from 1927 to 1946 and gained the unfortunate dis-

An advertisement for Maison Frida in Magyar utca,
Budapest's former red light district

tinction of holding the highest recorded hyper-inflation in
financial history—the exchange rate being around 460 oc-
tillion pengő to one US dollar.

By 1934 Budapest's nocturnal social life may not have
been as exotically varied as it was half a century earlier,
but it still had a great deal to offer a young man recently arrived from England. It was a city of just over a million in population in 1934. It had what were called in those
pre-star rating days, twelve first-class, fifteen second-class
and forty third-class hotels. In addition it offered the traveller twenty-eight museums, twenty theatres and ten ther-
mal baths. Five-hundred-and-fifty-nine kilometres of lines
of public transport were served by 1,760 tram cars, 215 motor buses and 1,410 taxis. Leigh Fermor favoured making
his way about the city on foot. The Buda set of young so-
cialites, introduced to him by the von Bergs, made regular
forays into the nightlife on offer across the Danube in Pest.
One of the main focal points for late-night revellers was at
20 Nagymező utca, the location of Budapest's most famous

The Arizona club interior

nightclub of that period, the Arizona. The young Leigh Fermor had already cut his drinking teeth at the bar of London's bohemian Cavendish Hotel and the even more raffish upper-class drinking establishment the Gargoyle Club. To him the Arizona would have been a home away from home, a sort of Budapest version of Waugh's 'The Old Hundredth' in *Brideshead Revisited*, with the Arizona's patroness, Mici Rozsnyai, as the reincarnation of Ma Mayfield. Mici and her husband, Sándor, opened the club just three years before Leigh Fermor arrived in Budapest and by 1934 it was already the epicentre of Budapest's sophisticated yet slightly louche nightlife. It was close to the city's main theatres and restaurants and stayed open long after other places of entertainment had closed for the night. Here, from *Between the Woods and the Water*, is surely one of the most engaging and enticing prose descriptions of a nightclub that makes one wish such places still existed. Coming from a party in Buda he 'whirled downhill across the Chain-Bridge to plunge into the scintillating cave of the most glamorous night-club I had ever seen. Did the floor of the Arizona really revolve?

The Arizona club exterior

It certainly seemed to. Snowy steeds were cantering around it at one moment, feathers tossing: someone said he had seen camels there, even elephants'.

While 'seeing pink elephants' is a delightful old sobriquet for having had one too many nightcaps, we may take him at his word. The Arizona had an arrangement with the nearby Budapest Zoo for hiring animals as part of their floor shows. It even had its own pet fox, who from contemporary footage of the club, seems to mix quite amicably with the clientele. Leigh Fermor thought he recognized a troupe of acrobats whom he had met and sketched in Vienna and were performing in the club during one of his visits. He was delighted to discover it was his old friends, the Koschka family of acrobats, who were providing the entertainment and 'pyramidally extant, glittering in apotheosis!' The club was technically very advanced for the period. The dance floor on which they performed did indeed revolve and rise and fall at the push of a button as did the tiered layers of circular cubicles containing the plush velvet seating and tables. Surrounding all this intoxicating glamour was a series of vast ostrich feather fans which waved gently up and down to cool the ardour of the dancers on the highly waxed dance floor.

The Arizona survived the conservatism of the Horthy regime but it did not survive the German occupation of Budapest and in 1944 the club was closed because it found disfavour with the Nazi guardians of the city's wartime morality. There was also the matter of the Jewish faith of its owner, Sándor Rozsnyai. He was arrested and sent to forced labour but despite the best efforts of his wife, who was not Jewish, he disappeared at the end of 1944. Mici disappeared soon after her husband, possibly killed by the Arrow Cross thugs who were purging the city of Jews and anyone else who found disfavour with their fascist ideology and Mici would certainly be high on that list. The Arizona died with the Rozsnyais. In 1988 the Rozsnyais, the Arizona and Budapest of the period were memorialized in Pál Sándor's movie *Miss Arizona*. Today 20 Nagymező utca is home to the *Mai Manó Ház*—the House of Hungarian Photography. After the closure of the Arizona, the building served as a school and also as a showroom for the Hungarian Motorists' Club. But there is sometimes talk in Budapest of some enterprising soul reviving this legendary pleasure dome.

What the young Leigh Fermor was witnessing in the 1930s was the last glory days of Budapest as one of Europe's most glamorous capital cities. His eyewitness account is at once a eulogy and an epitaph for a great city: 'Life seemed perfect: kind uncensorious hosts; resplendent and beautiful new friends against the background of a captivating new town; a stimulating new language, strong and startling drinks, food like a delicious bonfire and a prevailing atmosphere of sophistication and high spirits. [...] I was intoxicated by the famous delights of the place.'

He made a valiant and earnest attempt to learn Hungarian, a language so difficult it has been characterized as the only language for which the devil has any respect. He kept a Hungarian/English word list at the back of his diary of travel notes. Its contents reveal much about the company the socially ambitious young traveller was keeping on his journey. He makes special note of the Hungarian terms for the various ranks of the nobility and even for royalty.

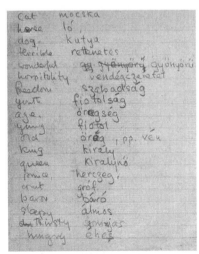

The Hungarian terms for the nobility carefully noted
in the back of PLF's 1934 diary

His ear was so finely tuned to this complex language, that fifty years after his first exposure to Hungarian, he still had in his aural memory phrases called out in doleful vocal arabesques by flower sellers on the Budapest quays: 'Virágot! Szép virágot!' (Flowers! Beautiful flowers!). And in doing so, he later recalled to Rudi Fischer, connected 'Virág' to the father of Leopold Bloom in James Joyce's *Ulysses*. For it was the Hungarian town of Szombathely which Joyce chose as the birthplace of Leopold Bloom's Jewish father, Rudolf Virág or Bloom. Leigh Fermor remembered too that it was a Sándor Blum who was the great Budapest maker of many of those splendid Hungarian army officers' uniforms he saw on his journey. He also recalled the plangent cries of the lovelorn in the Hungarian romantic ballad sung to him by a girl in Budapest: 'Érik a hajlik a búzakalász, / Nálamnál hűbb szeretőt nem találsz' (The ears of corn are ripening and swaying / A lover more faithful than me you will never find). Many years later it still irked him terribly he could only remember the opening line. He observed of the Hungarian language: 'On the printed page the fierce-looking sentences let slip no hint of their drift. Those tangles of S's and Z's! [...] I wondered if I would ever be able to exhort a meaning.' Out of a new friendship forged in Budapest he extracted the following understanding of the Hungarian language. 'Coming from a great distance and wholly unrelated to the Teutonic, Latin and Slav languages that fence it in, Hungarian has remained miraculously intact. Everything about the language is different, not only the words themselves, but the way they are formed, the syntax and grammar and above all the cast of mind that brought them into being. I knew that Magyar belonged to the Ugro-Finnic group, part of the great Ural-Altaic family. "Just", one of my new friends told me, "as English belongs to the Indo-European."' His inter-

locutor followed this up by saying that the language closest
to Hungarian was Finnish.

'How close?'
'Oh very!'
'What, like Italian and Spanish?'
'Well no, not quite as close as that....'
'How close then?'
Finally after a thoughtful pause, he said, 'About like
English and Persian.'

At the age of nineteen it was Hungarian as an instrument
of seduction and not of scholarly exegesis which Leigh Fermor was interested in. He was anxious to communicate
with the many beautiful girls he was encountering at parties and balls. There were also romantic meetings in a much
favoured restaurant of those days called 'Kakuk', which
means cuckoo in Hungarian. It was at 22 Attila körút in
the first district and much loved for the quality of its Gypsy music as much as for the quality of its food. It was in
the heart of the bohemian quarter called Tabán, the Mont-
parnasse of Budapest, which was in its twilight days when
Leigh Fermor visited. 'I crossed Tabán—a rainy watercol-
our. / I would be at peace here and maybe happy too,' the
poet Dezső Kosztolányi wrote of this place, which had
been inhabited since neolithic times and been developed
by the Romans and later the Turks as a place to take the
waters. Soon after Leigh Fermor left Budapest the Tabán
fell victim to the developer's wrecking ball and its bohemian community was dispersed. Nearby Leigh Fermor saun-
tered past on the west side of Batthyány tér the White Cross
Inn where Casanova stayed while taking the waters at the
nearby Rác baths. Legend has it that the famous Lothario

seduced a local girl, a butcher's daughter. When the girl's father discovered the affair, with sharpened butcher's knife in his hand, he is said to have run Casanova out of the city.

Budapest still had, in 1934, a café life to match that of Vienna or Paris. Leigh Fermor does not make much mention of the cafés of Budapest, save for one in Buda, *Ruszwurm*, which he describes but does not name. He does mention the Duna Palota and Gerbeaud in Pest both still functioning today. It would be impossible to have been as social as he was in Budapest in 1934 and not to have visited some of the legendary Budapest coffee houses which included the Centrál Kávéház and the New York, both places of legendary literary retreat and both now restored to their former architectural glory in post-Communist times.

One of the cafés he is most likely to have visited was the Belvárosi Kávéház, which was situated in one of the twin palaces named after Clotilde, Princess of Saxe-Coburg Gotha, by birth and an Archduchess of Austria by marriage to Archduke Joseph, son of the Palatine of Hungary. These

The Kakuk in the bohemian quarter of Tabán, where PLF was enchanted by the Gypsy music

Ruszwurm in Buda in 1934. PLF's favourite café in Buda

neo-baroque buildings flanked the Erzsébet híd, the Elizabeth Bridge, one of the conduits which gave Leigh Fermor
daily egress from Buda to Pest. Little did he know, at this
time, he would soon be dining further along in his journey
with Archduke Joseph of Austria, the son of the woman after whom these Budapest landmarks are named.

The Belvárosi Kávéház was founded by Egon Rónay's father Miklós and was one of several Hungarian gastronomic
enterprises owned by the family. Egon Rónay's daughter,
Esther, recalls Leigh Fermor corresponded with her father
long after the war and he 'was proud of the Belvárosi because unlike other Budapest coffee houses at that time it
had a very mixed clientele. Other Budapest coffeehouses
were known to be patronized almost exclusively by writers
or professionals of one type or another but the Belvárosi

had an eclectic clientele.' She also recalls the Belvárosi was
the first business to reopen in Budapest after the siege in
1945. Her father cobbled together a few tables and chairs
in the shattered building and served coffee to all comers,
including the Soviet military personnel. This saved his life
because he was later arrested by the Soviets and was on
the point of being sent to Siberia when one of his Soviet
guards remembered being served coffee by him and freed
him because he assumed he was 'obviously from the working class' and not a bourgeois 'enemy of the people'. Thus
began the journey to freedom for the author of the legendary eponymous food guides.

The Belvárosi Kávéház, owned by Egon Rónay's father Miklós

It was in the coffee houses of Budapest that the young
ladies who became the focus of Leigh Fermor's attention in
his final days in the city were mostly to be met and court-
ed. There was one girl in particular he was anxious to win
the attention of. Annamária Miskolczy was one of the Budapest beauties he met during the rounds of parties he at-

Painting of the Belvárosi Kávéház after the Siege of Budapest
by Kálmán Istokovits

tended. She was a student of art history and she acted as his guide around Budapest's many picture collections in between bouts of 'noctambulistic' socializing, as he liked to call it. Such were Annamária's social connections—her father Jenő was a very senior civil servant in the Horthy administration and her grandmother was Countess Etelka Markovits—that she was able to get herself and her young guest invited to the home of two of the city's wealthiest residents, and its greatest private art collectors: 93 Andrássy út, the home of Baron Mór Lipót Herzog von Csete. His brother-in-law, Baron Ferenc Hatvany, lived in a neoclassical villa in Buda. The two houses contained between them some of the most important paintings held in private hands anywhere in Europe. The Hungarian aristocracy had a well-established reputation throughout Europe as serious art patrons. The most important of such patronage was represented in the Esterházy collection, assembled in part from fabulous collections such as those of Borghese and Barberini. It was resplendent with representation of works by Rubens, Van Dyck, Correggio, Tintoretto, and Goya. Raphael's *Madonna* now known as the '*Esterházy Madonna*', was one of the most important pictures in the family collection, which, due to financial difficulties, was sold 'on generous terms' to the Austro-Hungarian state in 1870. Today it can be seen where Leigh Fermor viewed it in 1934 as part of the collection of the Museum of Fine Art in Budapest. Other aristocratic families, such as the Andrássy, Károlyi and Zichy, were at the forefront of Hungarian art patronage and were later joined by the emerging wealthy Jewish industrial magnates into whose ambit and whose houses and private collections Leigh Fermor was introduced by the well-connected Annamária Miskolczy.

The first house he visited, that of Baron Herzog, was spacious but had become so crowded with world-class art that by the time Leigh Fermor visited it, there was hardly any room left for the family. The walls of the room which served as Baron Herzog's study were hung shoulder to shoulder with major El Greco canvases. It was, without doubt, the

Baron Mór Lipót Herzog von Csete (back left)
and his family in happy times

Baron Herzog's study in Budapest showing some of his collection
of works by El Greco

greatest private collection of works by El Greco outside of
the Prado in Spain. It was also crammed full of other mas-
terpieces including works by Velázquez, Corot, Renoir,
Monet and Courbet. Sadly Leigh Fermor does not record if
the Baron was at home when he and Annamaria called. Mór
Herzog was dead seven months after their visit and within
ten years his famous art collection had fallen victim to plunder. Baron Herzog was Jewish.

After the Baron's death in November 1934, his collection
passed to his wife and remained under her care until her
death in 1940. It was then inherited by their three children,
Erzsébet, István and András, but with a view to keeping it
together as a collection. In 1942 as anti-Semitism gained an
increasing grip on Hungary, András Herzog, was arrested
and sent to a work camp for Jews where he died a year later.
When the Germans marched into Hungary in 1944, Ado-
lf Eichmann arrived not only to oversee the annihilation of
the country's Jews but to also to plunder their valuable possessions. It was at this time the paintings and other treas-

87

ures which the young Patrick Leigh Fermor admired in the house on Andrássy út in 1934 were stolen from the Herzog family. Today many of those paintings are still in the Hungarian Museum of Fine Art and form the core of the institution's Spanish collection. In 2010 David de Csepel, the great-grandson of Baron Herzog began legal action on behalf of the heirs to the Herzog estate for restitution of the family's property.

The story of the second house and private art collection which Leigh Fermor visited is equally (if not, indeed, more) tragic, than the first. Baron Ferenc Hatvany, brother-in-law of Mór Herzog, came from a wealthy Jewish family who made their fortune in banking and sugar refining in the nineteenth century. By the time Leigh Fermor visited his collection, it consisted of over 700 of the finest quality pictures with a strong emphasis on Old Masters and Hungarian pictures, but his real passion was for nineteenth-century French painting. Paintings by Ingres, Delacroix, Corot, Manet, Pissarro and Renoir hung on the walls of his villa

Baron Hatvany's villa in Buda where PLF visited his art collection

Interior of Baron Hatvany's palace showing part of his collection

in Buda, designed by Miklós Ybl, one of Hungary's most distinguished and prolific architects. Beside his French favourites hung works by Tintoretto and Constable. It may not have been the largest private collection in Budapest but many art historians agree that Hatvany's connoisseurship was so refined it was considered by many connoisseurs and art critics to be among the greatest of the private collections in Europe.

What made Hatvany's collection special was, he was not just another rich collector, but a trained artist. He studied art under the Hungarian artists Ármin Glatter and Sándor Bihari in Budapest. He spent time at the artists' colony at Szolnok and also studied in Paris under Jean-Paul Lurens at the Julian Academy, which produced, among other artists, Marcel Duchamp and Diego Rivera. Hatvany owned one of the most controversial paintings in the history of art. Courbet held a special affection for Hatvany and he was immensely proud of owning the notorious canvas *L'Origine du monde*. It is a close-up of a woman's genitalia and had been commissioned in the mid-nineteenth century by an Ottoman diplomatist and a truly cosmopolitan Oriental, Khalil Bey (Halil Şerif Pasha). The painting was lost to him in 1868 when he became undone by his ruinous gambling habits and was compelled to auction his extensive art collection in Paris. The controversial picture disappeared from view for nearly half a century until bought by Baron Hatvany from a Paris gallery in 1910. It was the pride of his collection. The Hatvany collection survived the turmoil of the Hungarian Communist revolution of 1918. The paintings, like those of the Herzogs, were confiscated by the revolutionary government of Béla Kun, but were returned to their owner after the collapse of the short-lived Hungarian Soviet Republic. In the interwar period they were seen by such visitors to the house as Thomas Mann and the young Patrick Leigh Fermor. Just a few years after Leigh Fermor's, visit when Hungary fell under the influence of Nazi Germany, things began to change radically for the Hatvanys.

After Hungary entered the war, and following the first Allied bombing of Budapest, Baron Hatvany finally understood the danger for his collection. He deposited about half of it in the vaults of three Budapest banks. The SS eventually occupied the Hatvany villa. Hatvany survived the occupation but his villa was looted and later bombed. The fate of his collection remained a mystery until the conclusion of the Cold War. Essentially, the collection was looted by the Nazis and then the Soviets and its pieces mostly shipped out of Hungary. Some pictures remain part of the national collections in Budapest. A Constable ended up in the Tate in London. Parts of the collection fell into the hands of local looters. Hatvany, before he left Budapest, paid a ransom for

ward as king of a reduced north-western Syria. Their son, Prince Ra'ad bin Zeid is the present claimant to the throne of Iraq. The Pasha's brother, Musa Cevat Şakir, known as 'The Fisherman of Halicarnassus', murdered their father over suspecting him of coveting his wife and was exiled to the then rural fishing village of Bodrum. Today he is revered there as the founding father of this now popular tourist enclave. For the traveller about to set off on the road to Constantinople, such an introduction made his journey, in his own words, 'something more than an abstraction'.

Before we leave him on the road to the Alföld—the Great Hungarian Plain—let us consider the impact this young man made on a sophisticated circle of people in a sophisticated city. Count István Pálffy ab Erdőd knew many of the families which the young Leigh Fermor met in Budapest and later in Transylvania. Pálffy is the stepson of Elemér Klobusiczky de Klobisicz et Zétény, known by the sorbriquet 'Globus'. He features prominently as 'István' in *Between the Woods and the Water* and was Leigh Fermor's closest Hungarian friend. We will encounter him later in Transylvania. Pista Pálffy points out the old Hungarian families' natural inclination towards Anglophilia. They also remembered the support lent to Hungary in the post-Trianon period by Englishmen such as Lord Rothermere, the most outspoken foreign critic of the break up of Hungary's territories.

In the case of the Transylvanian families, Pálffy says 'their isolation led them to embrace any interesting traveller and even though they had little money, there were still plenty of servants, food and bedrooms to accommodate an extra guest'. Though many of them were living on their past prestige rather than on their present investments, there was an all-pervasive air of munificence. What Leigh Fermor offered in Budapest and in Transylvania made him doubly welcome. He was a curious mix of geniality and genealogy. He had a natural interest in, and curiosity about, the history of these ancient families. He had charm and good manners. To the old he was attentive and mannerly and to the young he was exciting and handsome. He possessed an unusual quality for one so young, a quality which remained a steadfast part of his make-up all of his life and that was his ability to charm almost anyone he came into contact with. The 'almost' must be added as a qualification because there were some who saw his extraordinary, if somewhat ill-disciplined, quirky intellect and his often voluble conversation as rather showy.

His own view of the Transylvanian nobility with whom he so easily fell in with was very sympathetic. It fitted perfectly John Millington Synge's view of the decline of the Anglo-Irish: '[O]ne seems to feel the tragedy of the landlord class [...] and of the innumerable old families that are dwindling away. [...] The broken green-houses and mouse-eaten libraries. [...] Many of the descendants of these people have, of course drifted into professional life [...] or have gone abroad; yet, whatever they are, they do not equal to their forefathers.'

There was, however, another reason why Leigh Fermor was made welcome in the houses of so many Hungarian aristocrats. This was his mother's dubious claim to descent from the Hiberno-Austrian Counts Taaffe, a lineage the young Leigh Fermor can hardly be blamed for accepting as fact, the information came, after all, from his own mother's lips. It would be some years hence when he would discover that his mother was a total fantasist and Olympian fabricator of myths. '[S]o terrifying and destructive, [...] so full of odd delusions and manias' is how he later described her in a letter to his former lover Balasha Cantacuzène. If one were to choose a calling card to gain entry to the houses of the Hungarian and Transylvanian nobility, in 1934, he could hardly have chosen a better one than that of the ancient house of Taaffe. The family had been inextricably involved in the history of Central Europe for generations and as Habsburg loyalists had played an important role in the defeat of the Turks in Central Europe.

The fighting Irishmen of the Habsburg Empire, those swashbuckling soldier adventurers, gave Leigh Fermor a reason to be proud of his claim to this Irish ancestry on his mother's side. An Irish O'Donell [sic] was only one of two noblemen in the Empire to be allowed impale the Imperial Arms of Austria with his own. That honour fell to Count Maximilian O'Donell for saving the life of the young Emperor Francis Joseph when a botched assassination attempt was made on his life by a Hungarian journeyman tailor called János Libényi in 1853. The motive for the attack remains unclear but the result was the construction of Vienna's Votivkirche, which was built in thanksgiving for the Emperor's safe delivery from the Hungarian tailor's knife. Butlers, FitzGeralds, O'Neills, Maguires, O'Byrnes, O'Briens and O'Reillys were among the roll call of Irishmen who served the Empire. The seventeenth-century Irish Viscounts Taaffe, later created Earls of Carlingford, produced ten well-known officers in the service of the Empire over a hundred-year period. The family settled in Ireland early in the twelfth century. Viscount Francis Taaffe was born at Ballymote, County Sligo, in 1639. He joined the Habsburg army and distinguished himself at the Battle of Vienna in 1683 and was made a Knight of the Order of the Golden Fleece. He was the first of many celebrated Counts Taaffe of the Habsburg Empire. A Taaffe became a Page of Honour to the Emperor Ferdinand III, later becoming chamberlain to the Emperor, a Marshal of the Empire, and Privy Counsellor. Eduard Taaffe (1833–1895), Count Taaffe, Viscount Taaffe of Corren, Eleventh Baron of Ballymote in the Peerage of Ireland, was the son of Count Ludwig Patrick Johann Count Taaffe (1791–1855), who was Minister for Justice during the 1848 Hungarian revolution. This connection may have been overlooked by Leigh Fermor's more nationalistic and patriotic-minded Hungarian encounters in the kingdom, because all in all he seems to have been a very good egg and much liked by the Empire's minorities. This was all heady stuff for the young Leigh Fermor who was delighted, at this impressionable stage of his life, to take on board his fabricated heritage as presented by his mother.

As a child, another member of this ancient family, Eduard Taaffe, was chosen as a playmate for the young Archduke, later Emperor Francis Joseph. From boyhood he was destined for political greatness, a fate which indeed fell his way with considerable ease. There was also a strong Hungarian connection through his marriage to Countess Irma Csáky de Körösszeg et Adorján, who was from an old Hungarian family. In the late eighteenth century the Taaffe family acquired the estate of Ellischau near Silver Mountain in the Bohemian district of Klatovy in what was Czechoslovakia when Leigh Fermor was on his walk. Here the family built a votive chapel in honour of Saint Barbara and in the neighbouring Church of Saint Anthony constructed a tomb for the family. It was desecrated during Communism when local apparatchiks searched the coffins, looking for the women's jewellery and the men's hunting guns. It was one of those strange obsessions among young Communists functionaries that the nobility were always buried with their jewellery and their guns. 'A shroud has no pockets' is what the desecrators of these ancient funeral vaults usually discovered.

Ellischau Castle home to the Counts Taaffe in Bohemia

The penultimate and ultimate Counts Taaffe have tragi-comic stories worthy in their own right of great fiction and were suitable fodder for the genealogical fantasies of Leigh Fermor's mother. Henry, the twelfth viscount and son of the aforementioned Eduard, was one of those noblemen who were known in England during the Great War as the four 'traitor Peers of the Realm'. While the Dukes of Cumberland, Albany and Brunswick, because of their German lineage, were obvious targets for public opprobrium, the Twelfth Viscount Taaffe and Baron Ballymote was a lesser-known quantity. He was a serving officer in the Austro-Hungarian army and saw himself as one of the Irish 'Wild Geese'. These were the old Irish noble families forced to flee to the continent after defeat at the Battle of Kinsale in 1601 when the old Gaelic order was defeated in the last years of the reign of Elizabeth I. He too fell victim to the Titles Deprivation Act of 1917, after a correspondent to the letters pages of *The Times* wrote, in high patriotic indignation, that 'no reference appears to have been made to the fact that an Irish peer, Viscount Taaffe, the twelfth of that title, is said to be now serving, with his son, in the Austrian Army'. The writer added with considerable brio, Elizabeth I's famous remark that 'her dogs should wear no collars but her own'. To add to Henry's misfortunes, in 1919 the new Austrian republic abolished all titles of nobility, leaving him as ordinary Mr Taaffe, a fate which may not have bothered him as much as the loss of his lands during the land reforms following the Austrian defeat at war's end.

The ultimate Taaffe in the committal line, Henry's son, Richard, moved back to his ancestral homeland, Ireland, in the late 1930s. No longer in a position to maintain the Castle of Ellischau, he sold it. Under Communism it served several institutional functions, as was the usual fate of the houses of the nobility in the region in those times. He resided in a house on Baggot Street, in central Dublin, near his club, the Kildare Street Club, where his portrait still hangs in the dining room. He became a distinguished gemologist, discovering in one of Dublin's antique shops—which prior to the first Irish property 'development' era in the late 1960s used to line the old Liffeyside quays—one of the world's rarest gemstones. Taaffeite is a mauve to purple/red precious stone which bears Richard Taaffe's name after he discovered the first one in a box of Sri Lankan spinels in a Dublin shop in 1945. A million times rarer than a diamond, sadly for Richard Taaffe, its value was not reflected in its rarity. Count Taaffe died in Dublin in 1967.

One wonders if Leigh Fermor sought out his mother's 'relative' when rattling around the pubs of Dublin's Baggot Street with the historian Robert Kee and the poet Patrick Kavanagh in 1953? Count Taaffe would certainly have been known to Lady Oranmore and Browne, with whom Leigh Fermor was staying at Luggala, County Wicklow.

Coffins in the vault of the Taaffe family desecrated during Communism

Count Richard Taaffe. Portrait in the Kildare Street Club, Dublin

Her son, Gareth Browne, recalled that visit for me during one of my own stays at Luggala many years ago. He remembered that Daphne and Xan Fielding were also staying for Christmas of 1953, as was Lucien Freud. Daphne had just divorced the Marquess of Bath and married Leigh Fermor's great friend and wartime companion, Xan Fielding. Gareth also recalled seeing Leigh Fermor, in a moment of storytelling exuberance, accidentally knock down the actress Hermione Baddeley with a gesticulatory wave of his hand and, being completely unaware of having done so, carried on with his story. As an undergraduate at Trinity College, Dublin, the Taaffe house was pointed out to me by an older friend whose family lived on Baggot Street with the words, 'In that house lived one of the last of the noble line of Taaffe. We just sat under his portrait in the [Kildare Street] club but nobody here or elsewhere now remembers that they were once one of the most powerful families in the Habsburg Empire.'

Leigh Fermor, with his voracious appetite for history, must have had some idea the impact of dropping the name 'Taaffe' had on the many grand Hungarian families under whose mahogany he so readily planted his feet. All of this must have appealed hugely to his imagination. The family connection to the noble house of Taaffe may have been a matter of considerable fabrication by his mother, but it went down rather well in the castles of Hungary and Transylvania, where such a lineage made him very welcome. It required a great deal more than charm and good looks to breach the ha-has of the Hungarian nobility, even in the straitened economic times in which they were living in 1934. In fact, it was just this claim to Taaffe blood, according to Rudi Fischer, his Budapest mentor, which opened many castle doors to him on his journey. He told Fischer he had mentioned the connection in Bratislava, to Tibor von Thuroczy, the castle door-opener *par excellence.* It was he who passed the word on to his friends along Leigh Fermor's route. We can imagine the delight of this vivacious nobleman on discovering a wandering descendant of the great General Count Taaffe, the man who helped hold the Turks at bay in Central Europe. He could not possibly see him anything *other* than properly received while walking through Hungarian soil on his way to Constantinople. It was a matter of personal honour and duty. The question of class in the upper echelons of Hungarian society, at this time, was just as thorny an issue as it was in the England Leigh Fermor had left behind. Perhaps it was just as well then that his hosts did not realize he was quite a few rungs further down the carefully delineated class ladder than they thought he was, or we might never have had these wonderful portraits of the twilight years of the Hungarian ascendancy.

Leigh Fermor liked to compare the castles in which he was a guest in Transylvania to the decayed houses of the Anglo-Irish gentry in Waterford and Galway. In 1953, while he was a guest in the far from decayed, elegant house of Guinness heiress and legendary hostess, Oonagh Lady Oranmore and Browne, in Luggala, County Wicklow, he experienced the rough and tumble side of the Anglo-Irish gentry. The house party went to a hunt ball hosted by the Kildare Hunt. For some bizarre reason Leigh Fermor asked one of the pink-coated hearties if they buggered the fox after a kill. Other witnesses to the fracas at the ball have said it was because he was drunkenly boasting about his grand Irish roots.

That sort of behaviour was not easily tolerated among the scions of the Anglo-Irish families, many of whom had

Luggala, County Wicklow, where PLF was a house guest
during an incident at the Kildare Hunt Ball

survived intimidation by the IRA and had their houses
burned during the War of Independence and some of whom
felt they had paid a high price for staying on in Ireland after
independence. They saw themselves as being as 'Irish as the
Irish themselves' and were likely to be annoyed if they sus-
pected a claim to their lineage to be bogus, especially when
coming from a middle-class Englishman. The outcome was
a severe drunken punch-up between some members of the
hunt committee and Leigh Fermor. The end result was several stitches to his head when he was admitted to the emergency room of a Dublin hospital. In 1946, Gerald Durrell
described him in a letter to Henry Miller as 'a marvellous
mad Irishman'. However, the incident at the Kildare Hunt
Ball seems not to have put an end to the robustness of his
claim to Irish aristocratic ancestry. In reply to a letter from
Mark Odescalchi in 1987, he was still laying claim to Taaffe
ancestry: 'I even had a remote Irish relation who command-
ed a [brigade] of the Imperial Army under the Duke of Lor-
rain called Francis Taaffe. They settled in Bohemia.'

He did, perhaps, have a real claim to less grand Irish
blood than that of the Taaffes, something his mother—Muriel (she liked to be known as 'Æileen') Ambler—seems to
have kept secret from him. Or perhaps she simply had a convenient moment of amnesia while recalling the glory days of
the Taaffe's. Her great-grandfather (William) James Ambler,
has entered the pantheon of Muriel's genealogical fantasy
world as a warrant officer on board the HMS *Bellerophon*.
She claimed her father told her that her great-grandfather
was on the ship when Napoleon surrendered to her captain,
Frederick Maitland, after Waterloo. No trace of this man exists on any naval records for the HMS *Bellerophon*. He was
more likely to have been a builder from County Cork but
even this presents something of a genealogical quagmire as

extensive searches of the Irish records have, thus far, failed to produce him. For Muriel Leigh Fermor the boundary between fact and reality seems, at times, to have been a very thin partition. The best dreams of an ancient lineage are often had on beds of straw, though it must be said Muriel Leigh Fermor's bed, as the wife of Lewis Leigh Fermor, of the Geological Survey of India, and the daughter of Charles Ambler a prosperous Raj-era businessman and stone quarry owner near Calcutta, was considerably more comfortable than the average bed of that time While still very far from the First XI in the viceregal pecking order, Muriel's social status was far from lowly, though the haughty memsahibs, would have classified her as 'coming from trade', something which may have been at the root of her own snobbery and invention of a grand family history. In later life, Leigh Fermor came to rue the self-deception which underlay his mother's embarrassing delusion of noble roots, while continuing to exercise his own penchant for the nobility, which he had acquired in Hungary as a young man.

The Budapest Leigh Fermor left in 1934 was on the eve of becoming a very changed place. The Great War and the collapse of the Dual Monarchy had already wrought unimaginable vicissitudes on the city. However, progress was not at a standstill, in fact, quite the contrary. Air travel was restricted to Vienna until an international airport was started at Ferihegy in 1939, though it was not fully operational until after World War II. The brief period between the two wars saw considerable change in the industrial infrastructure of Budapest. In 1950 Angyalföld became the thirteenth district of Pest and manufacturing and milling prospered in that area of the city often under the skilful guidance of Jewish investors. The Újlipótváros in the same district became the Jewish intellectual heart of the city between 1927 and 1944. It took an intellectual of Jewish background, Antal Szerb, to deflate the middle-class aspirations of the residents of this new quarter of the city. 'Everything here is modern and uncomplicated and detached and uniform. The entire district is two rooms and a hall, its inhabitants concealing doggedly, youthfully and with élan the single honest truth of their tedious lives: that they, none of them have any money.' They may not have belonged to the ancien régime of Budapest society, but they were among the ones making a serious contribution to the intellectual life of the capital.

One of the most important survivors in Hungarian literary and artistic life was still being published during Leigh Fermor's stay in Budapest. It would be impossible to imagine the libraries of his hosts, especially given their liberal leanings, not having copies of the magazine *Nyugat* (The West) scattered about on tables. Founded in 1908, it ceased publication in 1941 but in the meantime it had introduced the Western trends in intellectual life to Hungary—symbolism, impressionism, new trends in poetry, prose and philosophy all found space within its pages. It found trenchant opposition in *Napkelet* (variously translated as Sunrise, Orient or The East), a right-wing ultra-nationalist magazine established with government money as a foil to the liberal *Nyugat* and edited by the stridently anti-Semitic writer Cécile Tormay. She was involved in one of the most scandalous lesbian intrigues of the 1920s. She was presumed to have had a lesbian relationship with Countess Eduardina Zichy, which was made public knowledge in 1925 when the countess' husband, Count Rafael Zichy, sought a divorce from his wife, citing in court that his primary reason for seeking a divorce was his wife's affair with Tormay. There is an amusing anecdote of how one Budapest aristo-

Cécile Tormay, doyenne of the right and a lesbian icon

cratic family discouraged Tormay's unwelcome attention to their very pretty daughter. The family invented a parlour game during which a raffle was fixed for Tormay to win. The prize was a toy monkey which played with its penis. Underneath, on the base of the monkey, was written, 'The monkey plays with its penis, as Tormay plays with hers.' The message had the required effect and Tormay stopped calling on the family. She spent the last decade of her life living with her 'companion', Countess Ambrózy-Migazzi. She delivered a tribute to Mussolini in Rome in 1932 on behalf of the Hungarian Women's League—a strong right-wing Christian organization. Il Duce presented Budapest with the most curious of tributes. He gave the city a marble column which used to stand in the Roman Forum, not in return for Madame Tormay's loyal address, but as a gesture of thanks for Hungary's help with Italy's endeavours in helping gain her freedom from Habsburg rule. It stands today in the garden of the National Museum.

The many innovative Hungarian writers published in the pages of *Nyugat* include Endre Ady, Gyula Krúdy, Attila József, and Sándor Márai, though some writers whose sympathies were more right-leaning, like the controversial Albert Wass (Count Albert Wass de Szentegyed et Czege) were also published in the magazine. The edition of *Nyugat* published the month of Leigh Fermor's arrival in Budapest contained an article on Hitler, which referenced Miksa Fenyő's earlier forebodings, a study of Dali, a review of a production of *Hamlet*, and several reviews of contemporary art exhibitions.

The literary sensation of 1934 in Budapest should have been the publication of *Prae*, a privately published novel by Miklós Szentkuthy, who was just seven years older than Leigh Fermor. It was a sensation only among the *literati*

Miklós Szentkuthy in the 1930s

who were in the vanguard of progressive Hungarian writers. To the uninitiated it remained, like James Joyce's *Ulysses*, to which it is often compared, a thing of great mystery. Antal Szerb was one of the few contemporary writers to appreciate its significance: 'There has not yet been a Hungarian book as intelligent as *Prae*. It skips lightly, playfully, ironically and in incomparably individual fashion around the highest intellectual peaks of the European mind. It will become one of the great documents of Hungarian culture that this book was written in Hungarian.' It was followed in 1935 by *The One and Only Metaphor*, which major Hungarian critics such as László Németh hailed as a masterpiece. Németh wrote: 'Szentkuthy's invention has the merit that he pries writing open in an entirely original manner. [...] Where everything was wobbling the writer either joins the earth-shaping forces, or else he sets up his culture-building laboratory over all oscillations. Seated in his cogitarium, even in spite of himself, Szentkuthy is brother to the bellicose on earth in the same way as a cloud is a relative to a plow in its new sowing work.'

Leigh Fermor's interests at this time lay in a world far distant from new literary trends. His enthusiasms were more focused on the past and the glory days of the Old Order and ancient Hungary. He was absorbed in, and passively recording, the history of a society not quite in the last spasms of its death throes, but not far from it. Understandably he was not recording the general economic decline of Hungary in this period and would have been unaware that by 1934, 19 per cent of Budapest's citizens lived in poverty. Unemployment had escalated from 5 per cent in 1928 to almost 37 per cent by 1934.

One of the last great social hurrahs for the Old Order was the coronation of Charles IV in Budapest in 1916. Nowhere are these events better described than in *The Phoenix Land*, a memoir by one of Hungary's most colourful statesmen, sometime Foreign Minister, author and cultural icon, Count Miklós Bánffy de Losoncz. It was Bánffy who masterminded the grand ceremonial rites for the crowning of Hungary's last king. Bánffy's Budapest and the lost ascendency of his own class are skilfully observed in his writing. Leigh Fermor later described the author in an introduction he wrote to the English translation of Bánffy's *Transylvanian Trilogy* as 'this deeply civilized man'. Bánffy was the type of Hungarian aristocrat who represented everything which was honourable and decent in the world of this decaying, sometimes self-centred feudal class, a class which had forever entered the consciousness of a young English traveller. Though Leigh Fermor never met Bánffy nor visited Bonchida (Bonţida), Bánffy's grand Transylvanian estate, he heard much talk of this man and his historic Transylvanian family in the houses in which he stayed, including talk of Bánffy's *Transylvanian Trilogy*, which is the preeminent swan song for the class among whom Leigh Fermor found so much hospitality during his journey across Hungary, the Banat and Transylvania. The destruction of Bánffy's own house, Bonchida, in Transylvania was a harbinger of things to come for the ascendancy in the post–World War II era and would reflect the fate of many noble houses in Transylvania and elsewhere on Leigh Fermor's journey. The destruction of its inestimably valuable contents was another matter altogether. A convoy of around twenty German army trucks was spotted by Allied aircraft, in late August 1944, leaving the ancient settlement of Bonchida, a village some thirty kilometres from Kolozsvár (Cluj) on the northwestern Transylvanian plateau. The airmen had been following the course of the Kis-Szamos River, whose right bank embraces the village. The pilots were emboldened by the change of circumstances which had seen Rumania enter the war on the Allied side following the briefly successful coup led by King Michael I on August 23, 1944.

The country was a key target for Allied bombing raids from 1943 because of the crucial oil and grain supplies provided for Germany and the Axis powers by the fascist regime of Ion Antonescu. It was not unusual, therefore, that what appeared to be a large German supply convoy, speeding westward, would make an excellent target for the Allied airmen. What was unusual, however, was the content of the trucks forming this supposedly ominous looking convoy. They contained not the usual supplies required for the waging of war but several centuries of Transylvanian, Hungarian and Central European history. Under the canvas covers of the German vehicles speeding away from Bonchida was part of the antiquarian library, silver, furniture, rare porcelain, oriental carpets and other treasures of a noble family who had established their seat at Bonchida in the late fourteenth century. Silver, furniture and paintings could be replaced but lost forever was much of the irreplaceable Bánffy family papers which chronicled the centuries of service given by distinguished soldiers, diplomats and governors of provinces. Lost too were the everyday estate records which chronicled the administrative history of Bonchida itself.

The last scion of the family to occupy Bonchida Castle, Miklós Bánffy, was not in residence at the time of the looting. The rape of Bonchida was his terrible reward for trying, in April 1943, to bring Rumania and Hungary into the war on the Allied side. The Germans were determined on the most odious revenge, for not only did they engage in wholesale looting of the contents of the castle, they also

Bonchida (Bonţida), country seat of Count Miklós Bánffy de Losoncz

spilled petrol at key points around Bonchida's ancient structure, with a view to obliterating, in a great conflagration, all traces of the house.

The plan to obliterate Bonchida was conceived in the Hotel New York (The Hotel Continental under Communism) in the market square of Kolozsvár. This architecturally eclectic building was taken over as the German military headquarters in Transylvania. Nearby stood the splendid eighteenth-century Bánffy palace, which fortunately escaped the ire of the departing Germans, who were determined on revenge on all who had hindered them. It would take more than fire and looting to destroy the indomitable spirit of a man like Bánffy, who could trace his ancestry back to a ninth-century chieftain and whose family was one of the leading families in the service of Transylvania since the Middle Ages. He was aware of the destruction of a large part of his family's history but hurried back into the eye of the storm to Transylvania to see if anything could be salvaged. But also to see if he could be of service in that part

Count Miklós Bánffy de Losoncz

of the world he loved most. He returned, not to the ruin of Bonchida Castle, but to the place of his birth, Kolozsvár, a city Leigh Fermor would falsely claim to have visited in curious circumstances during his stay in Transylvania. Bánffy remained trapped in Communist Rumania until 1949. His plaintive and deeply heart-rending letters asking to be allowed to leave make very sad reading. He was seriously ill and practically penniless. Eventually he received a visa to return to Budapest, where he died in 1950.

Members of the extended Bánffy family have received some of their old estates back under Rumania's restitution laws, following the fall of Communism. More than three quarters of a million claims have been submitted for numerous lost assets in Rumania. This has created in itself a legal quagmire which will keep generations of lawyers, as yet unborn, in business. Miklós Bánffy's daughter Katalin, for many years a resident of Tangier, regained possession of Bonchida. In Hungary there was no restitution of confiscated property to its rightful owners. Instead, a rather awkward voucher system was put in place whereby owners were given vouchers which could be cashed in for land up to a maximum value of five million forints or about 20,000 euro. As one heir to a large Hungarian aristocratic estate put it, 'we could, at best, buy a new car to replace centuries of history and tradition.' In Rumania many of the old families have been given at least part of their heritage back. They include members of the Apor, Bánffy, Barcsay de Nagybarcsa, Béldi, Bethlen, Haller, Horváth-Tholdy, Jósika, Kálnoky, Kemény, Kendeffy, Mikes and Teleki families.

Before leaving Budapest Leigh Fermor had an experience which left such an impression on him that he would become in later life one of the most enthusiastic exemplars of what is known to devotees as 'a clubman'. In a borrowed suit he lunched, with Count Ladomér Zichy, an authority on the Tartar invasion of Hungary, at the most prestigious gentlemen's club in Budapest. Ladomér Zichy was elected to membership just as Leigh Fermor arrived in Budapest. The Nemzeti Casino was the Budapest equivalent of White's in London; its membership drawn largely, though not exclusively, from among the aristocracy. At the time of its foun-

Exterior of the Nemzeti Casino

Nemzeti Club Interior where PLF dined with Count Zichy

dation, by Count István Széchenyi in 1827, Jews were not excluded from membership nor were they ever as is sometimes to this day inaccurately stated. It must be said, however, that they were few in number. The club was then situated in the former Cziráky palace on the corner of Kossuth Lajos utca and Szép utca. Though notorious for its late-night card games the name Casino referred to a club and not a gaming institution. Great fortunes were known to have changed hands in this famous aristocratic retreat in the past but by 1934 the stakes were rather more modest. The membership list at this time was still representative of the majority of Hungary's old families but by then most tended to work for a living as lawyers and civil servants and not as owners of vast estates.

The Club building at 5 Kossuth Lajos utca was obliterated by a bomb during World War II exactly ten years after Leigh Fermor's visit. Many of its members fell victim to the war, several dying in bombing incidents in Budapest, others being forced into exile abroad or into internal exile. Two members died in Nazi concentration camps, the diplomat

Andor Szentmiklósy and the man who had been Mayor of Budapest in 1934, a highly decorated veteran of the Great War, Aladár Huszár. Both were anti-Nazi activists, Huszár, an ardent Hungarian nationalist was especially well known for his anti-Nazi articles in various Budapest publications. At least nine other members of the Nemzeti Casino were sent to either Dachau or Mauthausen, including wartime Prime Minister, Miklós Kállay, Count György Apponyi, Aladár Szegedy-Maszák, Ferenc Keresztes-Fischer, Gustav Gratz and Count Antal Sigray all of whom were strongly anti-Nazi and involved in efforts to get Hungary to switch to the Allied side.

Patrick Leigh Fermor left Budapest with treasured memories of a city on the cusp of great change. He went on to live a life crammed with incident and though it took him far from the friends he made in Budapest in 1934, the city would remain forever impressed on his memory. The next time he returned the best part of half a century had passed and the lives of his Hungarian friends had been utterly altered by war, by Communism, by revolution, and indeed in some cases by their own folly. His later return to Budapest was greatly motivated by a desire to see an old friend.

# II

# Across the Alföld
## The Great Hungarian Plain

*There is something primeval about those plains of Hungary
in the setting sun, as though the humanity inhabiting them
were still in the Biblical stage.*

Walter Starkie, *Raggle-Taggle*

On April 13, Leigh Fermor left Budapest and headed
south-east in the direction of the Rumanian border. Half
a century later, when he was publishing his account of this
part of the journey, his greatest fear was that it might be
bleached of colour and calcified into a 'plodding along
the road' account, unless he altered the facts to 'enliven
the narrative'. He warns the reader of this himself: 'I said
to myself that I was not writing a travel guide and that
these things don't matter, and from then on I let the tale
unfold.' He writes of borrowing a horse through the good
offices of Tibor von Berg who, one morning during his
Budapest stay, discreetly tested his young guest's riding
skills in a military stables outside Pest. He immortalized
this mount as Malek, 'a fine chestnut with a flowing mane
and tail, one white sock, a blaze and more than a touch of
the Arab to his brow'. This animal was waiting, he writes,
'by a clump of acacias on the Cegléd Road'. He began his
journey towards the Great Hungarian Plain, not mounted
on Malek, but on foot. He admitted, years later, to his biographer Artemis Cooper, that he fabricated this romantic element and that he had picked Malek up later into the
journey, impishly adding to this confession, 'You won't let
on, will you?'

Even in the simple act of borrowing a horse Leigh Fermor was the fortunate recipient of largesse from yet another of Hungary's grandest families. The horse was borrowed from a member of the Szapáry family whom he does not name in the book but from a list of addresses at the back of his Green Diary which he kept on the journey we may safely assume that the horse was picked up at the Szapáry's castle at Alberti Irsa (Albertirsa since 1950) which was on his way through the Puszta. The Diary names Countess Constance Szapáry with an address at this castle so she was, most likely, the connection for the hand over of 'Malek'. The Szapáry's townhouse in Budapest was at 14 Uri utca, across the street from the von Bergs'. Malek was stabled at their country estate. The benefactor was Count Gyula Szapáry, whose son, György became Hungary's ambassador to the United States in 2010. Malek's owner, as a 'class enemy', was later deported to Polgár by the Communist government in 1951 and left Hungary for good in 1956. His father, Count Gyula Szapáry de Szapár Muraszombat et Széchy-Sziget, had been Prime Minister of Hungary towards the end of the nineteenth century and his mother, Karolina Festetics, was from one of Hungary's grandest and wealthiest though not most ancient princely families. Princess Michael of Kent's mother was a member of the Szapáry family. Count Frigyes Szapáry de Szapár was the Austro-Hungarian ambassador in Saint Petersburg at the outbreak of the Great War. In 1998, Yad Vashem recognized Countess Erzsébet Szapáry as Righteous among the Nations for her role saving thousands of Jews in Budapest during World War II.

His association with the Hungarian nobility was suspended, if only briefly, as his journey took him further along the Alföld or the Puszta, as the Hungarians favour calling it—the Great Hungarian Plain. Outside Cegléd he en-

countered an old Hungarian peasant woman whose granddaughter hospitably gave him a glass of cold milk while he
tried to explain to the old woman, in broken Hungarian,
that he was an Englishman. His next encounter was with a
group of gypsies with whom he established his customary
easy rapport, offering wine and attempting to engage them
in conversation using elements of Hindi. One can only assume his knowledge of Hindi, no matter how scant, came
from his father Dr Sir Lewis Leigh Fermor, who worked
with the Geological Survey of India in Calcutta. His maternal grandfather, Charles Ambler, also had an association with India, where he was the owner of a slate and stone
mine outside Calcutta. It was a custom among many Raj
families to use phrases from the languages of the sub-con-
tinent in conversation at home. But his father was rarely at
home and his son never visited him in India. Whatever the
source of the young Leigh Fermor's Hindi, it stood him in
good stead with this band of gypsies, with whom he spent
an unhindered night before moving on to enjoy the next

All that remains today of the Szapáry Castle at Alberti Irsa
where PLF collected his mount

PLF not on 'Malek' but later in Moldavia

introduction offered him by his Hungarian aristocratic ac-
quaintances. Leigh Fermor had many pleasant encounters
with gypsies in the course of his journey. It has long been a
source of interest as to how the gypsies first came to and settled in Hungary. In 1455 the great János Hunyadi, defender
of the kingdom against the Ottomans, acceded to a request
from a Transylvanian nobleman, Tamás Barcsay, to allow
the settlement of four gypsy serf families on his lands. This
is the first recorded instance of gypsies being allowed the
right of permanent settlement in the Kingdom of Hungary.

The town of Szolnok was Leigh Fermor's next destination. Situated on the banks of the Tisza River, it lies at the
epicentre of the Great Hungarian Plain, about a hundred
kilometres south-east of Budapest. Szolnok's history is both
ancient and tragic. It supports, to this day, one of the first
purpose-built artists' colonies in Hungary, founded in 1902.
It was occupied by the Ottomans, the Rumanians, bombed
by the British and the Americans during World War II, and
used as a clearing centre for Hungarian Jews being deported to Mauthausen in 1944.

In Szolnok, Leigh Fermor was accommodated by Dr Imre Hunyor de Vizsoly. He was Deputy Head of the City Administration of Szolnok until 1928 but thereafter practiced as a lawyer. What really interested Leigh Fermor about him was that he had been educated at the Ludovica Academy in Budapest—the Sandhurst of Hungary—and had a military career in Szombathely with a hussar regiment before becoming a lawyer in Szolnok and later in Budapest. Imre Hunyor was thirty-four when Leigh Fermor met him. His legal practice was sufficiently prosperous to later warrant having an office in the very prestigious Klotild Palace in Budapest's fifth district. His social connections were such that he was invited as a guest to the wedding of King Zog of Albania to the Hungarian Countess Geraldine Apponyi, whose lawyer and friend he was. Dr Hunyor brought as his wedding gift a gypsy band from Budapest. The Albanian Queen's kinswoman, Countess Julia Apponyi, was not invited at Zog's insistence, her son Pista Pálffy recalled, because she had a dress shop in Budapest and was therefore 'in trade'. Zog chose to ignore the fact of her ancient lineage and her close relationship to the British monarch. Zog reigned as King for nine years from 1928. Zog had earlier hoped to marry another of Leigh Fermor's Hungarian aristocratic contacts, Countess Hannah Mikes, a member of an ancient and distinguished Transylvanian family. In the end she did not tie the nuptial bonds with the Albanian monarch. After a brief visit for a potential suitability inspection Hannah Mikes returned to Hungary with the gift of an emerald necklace. As the niece of Count Bethlen, one of the undisputed champions of Hungarian irredentist claims in Transylvania, her marriage to a Balkan monarch was opposed by Rumania and Yugoslavia.

Imre Hunyor was just the sort of Hungarian gentleman which the young Leigh Fermor greatly admired. He had an

Imre Hunyor as a cadet at the Ludovica
Academy, Budapest, 1918

upright military bearing, was an excellent horseman and had a vast library of 5,000 volumes in his Szolnok residence. The house was of the type Leigh Fermor would experience many times along his journey. Its elegant L-shaped form was single storied, had a wraparound veranda and was built over a basement and set in large gardens facing the old artists' colony of Szolnok. The Hunyors had been granted their patent of nobility in 1625 when Tamás Hunyor de Vizsoly was ennobled by the Prince of Transylvania and two years later (in 1627) by the Habsburg Emperor. The family takes it name after the town in north-east Hungary where the first translation of the Bible—by the Protestant Bible pastor Gáspár Károli—was printed in Hungarian in 1590.

Leigh Fermor settled in quite comfortably in the Hunyor household. Imre Hunyor's wife, Kató, spoke English and German, and as was his usual practice he availed himself of the use of their extensive library. The garden of the house ran down to the Tisza River and meals were taken on the veranda. In the Hunyor's guest book, which still survives in the family, he signs as 'Michael Leigh-Fermor' just as he did in Budapest in the von Berg's guest book. He gives a Mayfair address and telephone number of his lodgings.

Two years after Leigh Fermor left the Hunyor's house the family sold the property and moved to Budapest. In a little more than a decade after his departure the family's wealth and position in Hungarian society would be devastated by the brutality of the new Communist administration. Before this happened Imre Hunyor himself was arrested and imprisoned by the Nazis in 1944. His name was on a blacklist because he objected to the anti-Jewish laws which prohibited Jews from practicing law in Hungary and he resigned from the bar in protest. In the spring of 1948 all of the family's goods, their apartment, their 5,000 books, their money and even the money of Imre Hunyor's clients was taken by the Communist state. The family was split up, he was not allowed to practice law as a 'class enemy'. Eventually, in 1956, his wife and daughter were able to make good their escape from Hungary to settle first in Rome and later in South Africa. Imre Hunyor died in Budapest in 1971, a dignified figure who survived the rigours of Communism by maintaining his dignity in a quiet manner as so many of his class did. Leigh Fermor would be reunited with Imre Hunyor's daughter Katharina—a small child at the time of his visit—in Budapest over fifty years later.

When Leigh Fermor was set to move on from Szolnok, Dr Hunyor contacted his neighbour the enigmatic 'Baron

Detail of painting of the Hunyor's house (c. 1934)

Schossberger' to whom he had a letter of introduction. He does not call him anything other than 'Baron Schossberger' in *Between the Woods and the Water* but he does mention that he 'came of a wealthy Jewish banking family in Budapest' and was living on an estate in a 'low country house' near Mezőtúr. The land registry for Szolnok County does not show a Baron Schossberger owning or renting land in the area in 1934. However, Imre Hunyor's daughter, Katharina, remembers a Schossberger family living nearby. He may have confused the Baron from another part of his walk. The veracity of the narrative is not, as we have already seen, etched in stone and it is often all the better for engaging the occasional *madeleine* rather than relying on hard fact.

However, the fact he had encountered a member of the Schossberger family is in itself interesting. The head of the family was Baron Sigmund Schossberger de Tornyai, the son of a Jewish trader, Lazar Schossberger from Moravia. They were industrialists and bankers in Budapest and fabulous-

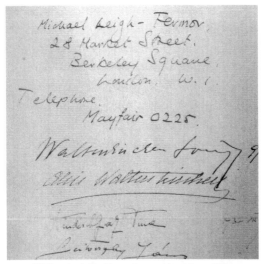

PLF's entry in the Hunyor's guest book from 1934

ly wealthy. Until the 1850s Sigmund worked with his father and then branched out on his own. He became the first Jewish member of the Hungarian upper house and was created a baron by Emperor Franz Joseph. Sigmund's daughter, Jenny (Eugénie), was the mother of George de Hevesy, Nobel laureate in chemistry in 1943. His brother Paul Bischitz de Hevesy was a diplomat in the Austro-Hungarian Foreign Service. Their grandmother, Johanna Bischitz de Hevesy, the daughter of Herend porcelain manufacturer Móric Fischer, was one of Budapest's greatest philanthropists. Her efforts to help Budapest's poor was honoured by the Austrian Emperor, the King of the Belgians and most especially by the poor of Budapest. When she died thousands of the city's poor, Jewish and Christian alike, turned out for her funeral.

In 1873 Baron Schossberger bought lands from the Esterházy family in Tura which lies just east of Budapest between the Great Plain and the Mátra Hills in the Galga valley. There he built a French Renaissance style castle, possibly

to a design by the Hungarian architect Miklós Ybl. There
is some debate among architectural historians as to the exact hand responsible. The family continued to prosper until the introduction of a series of anti-Jewish laws in Hungary in the 1930s, which greatly affected the economic clout of
Jewish families like the Schossbergers. They were forced to
hand over, and to sell through compulsory purchase, thousands of hectares of their lands. The Schossberger castle was
occupied by Soviet soldiers during World War II. It became
a military hospital in 1945 and later a school. Its more recent
fate has seen it sold to a business consortium which appears
to have somewhat long-term plans to turn it into a hotel.

Leigh Fermor's next halting point was the ancient settlement of Gyoma, today known as Gyomaendrőd (the two
small towns of Gyoma and Endrőd were united in the early 1980s). Destroyed during the Ottoman Wars, Gyoma was
rebuilt by Hungarian Calvinists in the eighteenth century.
There he had an introduction to Dr vitéz Gyula Haviar. '*Vitéz*', meaning gallant or valiant soldier, was a Hungarian order founded by Admiral Horthy to honour soldiers after the
debacle of the Great War. Soldiers of distinction were giv-
en grants of land and the honorific '*vitéz*' was placed before
their name. Dr Haviar who had been a soldier of some distinction was now a lawyer and was in the long line of such
former military men to whom Leigh Fermor had been giv-
en introductions. He describes him thus:

> Dr. vitéz Haviar Gyula was tall, dark and slightly eastern-
> looking with heavy-lidded eyes, a swooping nose, high
> narrow temples and a rather sad smile. I wondered if he
> could have been of Armenian descent: numbers of these,
> respected for their nimble wits and teased for their prom-
> inent noses, were scattered about the country like little

The fairytale Schossberger house at Tura today

gatherings of toucans. But it wasn't an Armenian name, nor yet Hungarian. Rumanian names originating in a profession—equivalent of 'Potter' or 'Tyler'—sometimes ended in -ar, but not here, I think: well-known engravings of Kossuth and Deák hung in his drawing room and apart from the not very fluent German in which we conversed, Magyar was his only language.

After a relaxing dinner in the town with Dr Haviar and his family, he departed the next day but not before he drew a portrait of the *vitéz*'s ten-year-old daughter, Erzsi (whom he mispelled Erszi). He gives an enchanting account of this little minx:

Erzsi ran off excitedly to tidy her hair. When she was still not back after ten minutes, they gave her a shout and she arrived looking extraordinary in a cloche hat of her mother's, long ear-rings and a fox stole; she had covered her face with powder and had turned her lips into a sticky Cupid's bow. Perching on a tuffet, she crooked a bangled wrist on her hip while her other hand flourished a twelve-inch ciga-rette-holder and tapped off the ash with vampish languor. It was convincing and rather eerie, an advanced case of lamb dressed up as mutton. 'Isn't she silly?' her mother said fondly. I'm not sure the sketch did her justice.

Leaving Gyoma behind, he followed the course of the Sebes (fast flowing) Körös River, until he reached the ancient settle-ment of Körösladány. There he made his way to a long-house, called rather grandly a castle or *kastély* in Hungarian, sug-gesting a castle in the English sense but in fact being long, low manor houses usually with aggrandizing pillared porti-cos added to the front. The occupants of this house were, in the eyes of the young traveller, amongst the grandest, though certainly not of the most ancient in lineage, of his Hungari-an hosts. He delighted in the fact that the Counts von Mer-an were descended from a Habsburg Archduke. His host, Count Johann 'Hansi' von Meran, was the great-grandson of Archduke Johann of Austria, the son of Emperor Leopold II of Austria, Holy Roman Emperor. Hansi von Meran's great-great-grandmother was Maria Luisa de Borbón, the Infanta of Spain. The count's archducal great-grandfather married Anna Marie Josephine Plochl, daughter of Jakob Plochl, a postmas-ter from Bad Aussee in Styria on September 3, 1823, in a mor-ganatic and secret marriage which caused quite a scandal in Imperial court circles of the time and temporarily estranged him from his family. Anna Marie was first granted the title Baroness von Brandhofen and later Countess von Meran. She and the archduke were the parents of Franz Count von Meran from whom Leigh Fermor's host at Körösladány descended.

In *Between the Woods and the Water*, he explains, with great gusto, the background of his host's illustrious ancestor:

Archduke Johann was the most interesting of them. He courageously led an army against Napoleon at the age of eighteen, governed provinces with wisdom and justice and was often called to high office at critical times. Intelligent, determined and steeped in the principles of Rousseau, he was a lifelong opponent of Metternich and his passion for the simplicities of life in the mountains made him a sort of uncrowned king of the Alps from Croatia to Switzerland. In the romantic picture in my room, made about 1830, he was leaning on an alpenstock among forested peaks, a fowling piece on his shoulder, and a broad-brimmed wide awake was thrust back from a thoughtful brow. What a relief to record the qualities of these Habsburg paragons! Courage, wisdom, capacity, imagination and a passion for justice led them in ways deeply at variance with the ill-starred fortunes of their dynasty, and this particular prince put the final touch to his abhorrence of the capital by a morganatic marriage to the daughter of a Styrian postmaster. She and their children were given a title from what was then Meran, in the South Tyrol, now Merano in the Alto Adige.

His von Meran hosts were thirty-eight-year-old Count Johann von Meran, who married in 1919, Countess Ilona Almásy de Zsadány et Törökszentmiklós, a member of the family from which hailed László Ede Almásy, the eccentric Hungarian desert explorer inaccurately portrayed in *The English Patient* as decidedly heterosexual and incurably romantic. The real character was most certainly not the former, however, as a fearless desert explorer we must certainly grant him the latter part of the description as a suitable sobriquet.

The von Meran House at Körösladány at the time of Leigh Fermor's visit

The von Meran House at Körösladány. Today it is the village schoolhouse

Ilona von Meran and her family he describes as the perfect example of gracious hosts:

> She was charming and good-looking with straight, bobbed fair hair—I think it must have been parted in the middle for it was this, a few years later, that reminded me of her when I met Iris Tree. She wore a white linen dress and espadrilles and had a cigarette-case and a lit cigarette in her

hand. 'So here's the traveller,' she said in a kind, slightly husky voice and took me through a french window to where the rest of her family, except her husband, who was due back from Budapest next day, were assembled round tea things under tall chestnut trees whose pink and white steeples were stickily bursting out. I can see them gathered like a conversation piece by Copley or Vuillard, and can almost catch their reflection in the china and silver. They were Countess Ilona Meran, just described, a son and daughter called Hansi and Marcsi, about thirteen and fourteen, and a much smaller girl called Helli, all three of them very good-looking and nice-mannered and a little grave. There was a friend, perhaps a relation, called Christine Esterházy.

He seems to have had some interest in Countess Esterházy because he added her name to the burgeoning list of aristocrats at the back of his diary which by then was beginning to resemble his personal edition of the *Almanach de Gotha*. But then it would be surprising if he were not interested in her because she came from one of the grandest families in Hungary. The Esterházy de Galántha family were ennobled in the Middle Ages and in the early eighteenth century were made princes of the Holy Roman Empire. It would have been near impossible for him not to have heard talk of this ancient family during the course of his visits to Hungarian country houses. They were amongst the greatest art collectors in Europe and patrons of composers, particularly Joseph Haydn.

Christine Esterházy was staying with the von Meran's during Leigh Fermor's visit. There were three children in the family: Marcsi von Meran, born Maria Ladislaja Helene von Meran in 1920; her brother Hansi, Johann Baptist von

Meran, born in 1921; and their baby sister Helli, Helene von
Meran, born in 1927. He would encounter them again many
years later in much altered circumstances. The exalted social status of his hosts was evident from some of the engravings in his bedroom and, as ever, Leigh Fermor was a keen
observer of social standing:

> Once again, pictures in my room put me on the track. One
> of these showed Archduke Charles, flag in hand, charging
> the Napoleonic army through the reeds of Aspern. (His
> statue opposite Prince Eugene on the Heldenplatz in Vien-
> na shows him at the same moment, on a frenetically rear-
> ing steed. How surprised he would have been! He had re-
> fused all statues and honours during his lifetime.) I had
> first become aware of him when I gazed across the Dan-
> ube at the Marchfeld after leaving Vienna: it was there, a
> few miles from Wagram, that the battle, the first allied vic-
> tory over Napoleon, was fiercely fought and won. The next
> print showed his brother, the subject of that endless song
> in deep Styrian dialect called the Erzherzog-Johanns-
> Lied: I had first heard it at an inn opposite Pöchlarn and
> often since. These brothers, two of many, were grandchil-
> dren of Maria Theresa, nephews of Marie Antoinette, and
> sons of Leopold II; and their elder brother, who succeeded
> as Francis II, was the last Holy Roman Emperor. (Lest Na-
> poleon should attempt to usurp it, he gave up the stupen-
> dous honour and became Emperor of Austria, just over a
> thousand years after the crowning of Charlemagne.)

In 1942 János von Meran was called up and served in the
Royal Hungarian Army on the Subcarpathian front. In
1944 he was taken prisoner by the Red Army. In his absence and as the front approached in late 1944, his fami-

The von Merans' ancestor, Archduke Johann of Austria

ly fled Körösladány for another property the von Merans owned in western Hungary. Two faithful retainers, a valet and a gardener, were left in charge of the house. Despite their best efforts, they were unable to prevent the building from being looted by the locals. Even to this day one often hears that it was 'the Russians' or 'the Germans' who looted all the grand houses in Hungary but all too often the local villagers were at the forefront of the looting.

On October 7, 1944, a Soviet army command took over most of the house, the rest was used as a field hospital. It was throughout this time that the library of 32,000 volumes was dispersed and disappeared. Most of the rare leather bindings were used as boot-mending material and the pages of ancient tomes used as lavatory paper. The Soviets left the building on October 29, 1945. An inventory of the contents of the house taken a few months later was only half a page long. Almost everything—paintings, silver, furniture, the priceless family archive, and all decorative elements had disappeared. A writing table used by Leigh Fermor in the library was one of the few objects to survive.

Countess von Meran and her children returned to their former home in December 1945. They were assigned three rooms in their own house by the National Aid Agency which had previously settled sixteen indigent (or perhaps politically well-connected) families in the building. Empty rooms were used as a granary. Dismantled Biedermeier doors were employed to transport agricultural produce into the building.

In June 1946, the von Merans' house was handed over to the local Agricultural Co-operative. Then as a result of some bureaucratic whim it was taken away from them and given to the Ministry of Education. It was at this point that the von Merans were dispossessed of their remaining three rooms in the house and told to move to a room in the former estate manager's house.

In the summer of 1948, after an absence of four years, Count János von Meran returned from Soviet captivity in Georgia. Three years later, in 1951, his old house, was given a new function as a local school—a function it still performs today.

Though reluctant to leave the von Merans at Körösladány, Leigh Fermor felt obliged to move on. On his last day of his stay there was some light-hearted speculation by the Countess about her husband's chances of being placed on the throne of Hungary in the unlikely event of a restoration of the monarchy. "'When there was all that fuss and talk a few years ago," the Countess speculated, "about who should be King, I couldn't help thinking"—and here she nodded in the Count's direction—"Why not him?" Her husband said, "Now, now!" disapprovingly, and after a few seconds, laughed to himself and went on with his paper.'

And with this engaging piece of family royal speculation put to bed, Leigh Fermor moved on to yet another stately *schloss* and to the first of a trio of aristocrats from the noble house of Wenckheim.

The Wenckheim family may not have been the oldest Hungarian aristocratic family with whom Leigh Fermor stayed but they certainly were among the most interesting. The comital branch came to prominence and great wealth in the eighteenth century. One member had already distinguished himself in the wars against the Turks and was raised in the peerage. Like the Habsburgs, the Wenckheims believed in marrying well to sustain and expand their land holdings. From the eighteenth century onwards Wenckheims married into nearly all the major Hungarian noble families from the princely to the baronial. It sometimes meant marriage between first cousins. The Wenckheims were once amongst the wealthiest landowners in the Empire. But by the time Leigh Fermor stayed with them they were feeling the financial pinch like so many other Hungarian landowners. The Wenckheim estates on the Puszta had as their managing agent, Béla Bartók's brother-in-law, Emil Oláh Tóth, who was married to Bartók's sister Erzsébet. Bartók recorded many folk songs from the workers on the Wenckheim lands.

By 1927 the family had already sold the Wenckheim Palace in Budapest to the municipality. The great neo-baroque house had already been turned into the Association of Joiners in 1919 during the short-lived Hungarian Soviet Republic of Béla Kun and later into the Museum of the Proletariat—a less appropriate use for this baroque masterpiece is unimaginable. Today it houses the Ervin Szabó Library. Szabó—born Samuel Armin Schlesinger—translated the works of Marx and Engels into Hungarian. It was one of the few houses in Budapest considered grand enough to entertain the Emperor to dinner on a regular basis.

The first of the three Wenckheim Puszta estates Leigh Fermor arrived at was near Vésztő, which was owned by a cousin of the von Merans, Count Lajos Mária Rudolf Dénes Frigyes József Wenckheim (to distinguish him from the other Wenckheims we are about to meet). 'I found him strolling in the avenue that led to the house. He must have been about thirty-five. He had a frail look, a slight tremor, and an expression of anguish—not only with me, I was relieved to see—which a rather sorrowful smile lit up. A natural tendency to speak slowly had been accentuated by a bad motor-crash brought about by falling asleep at the wheel. There was something touching and very nice about him, and as I write, I am looking at a couple of sketches in the back of my notebook; not good ones, but a bit of this quality emerges.'

He was alone in the house except for the servants. His wife Maria, a Teleki countess, was away—possibly because she was expecting their first child, Rudolf. He had already been married to Mária Pálma Hoffmann, who had rather formed the habit of marrying into the nobility, counting a Bethlen and a Máriaffy among her husbands. Leigh Fermor portrays him as a rather introverted character with a passion for bird life. 'He loved birds and had a way with them, for these two [a pair of exotic birds] followed him up the steps with a stately pace, then through the drawing room and the hall to the front door and, when he shut it, we could hear them tapping on it from time to time with their beaks.'

Wenckheim Palace Budapest exterior with Rothermere fountain (c. 1934)

Interior of Wenckheim Palace, Budapest

Count Wenckheim was rather amusing about the proliferation of comital titles in Hungary. He explained in a hu-
morous manner to Leigh Fermor the reason for the existence of so many barons and counts. Later in the journey, in
Transylvania, he meets Robert von Winckler, who is represented as the 'Polymath of the Wachau' and used as a sort of
scholarly *deus ex machina*, finding a place in different stages
of the narrative when the plot needs to be unravelled. 'The

Count Lajos Wenkheim sketched by PLF in 1934

polymath of the Wachau was very entertaining about this
proliferation of prefixes, including his own. 'Count and earl
are more or less equated,' he said, 'so if Tennyson's Lady
Clara Vere de Vere had been born in this part of the world,
she could easily have been the grandmother of a hundred
earls, instead of merely their daughter—with a bit of luck,
of course. Ten sons, with another ten apiece. There's a hundred for you—instead of only one, as in England.'

Count Wenckheim's daughter, Jeanne-Marie, married Christopher Charles Dickens, a direct descendant of Charles Dickens. Their daughter Catherine Dickens recalls the family memory of her grandfather as 'a jovial but practical man'. He had the foresight to pack up some of the family silver, which Leigh Fermor would have dined off in 1934, on the eve of the advance of the Soviet army through his estates ten years later. Within a few years he died in exile in Bregenz aged only 49. His wife died two years before him. His rather laconic sense of humour, referred to by his granddaughter Catherine, was evident in his parting remark to his young guest. "'Yes," he said, "there are lots of us *aber wir sind wie die Erdäpfel, der beste Teil unter der Erde*"—"We are like potatoes, the best part is underground."' Today this branch of the family's fortune has been restored by the acquisition by Lajos's son Rudolf, known as Engelbert, of one of Vienna's oldest breweries, Ottakringer. He was born in Budapest in 1934 but made his career in the brewing industry in Austria. His daughter Krisztina (Christiane) succeeded her father to the chairmanship of the board.

Returning to the rather scholarly figure of Lajos alone on the Puszta; he asked Leigh Fermor to stay on at Vésztő but he felt uncomfortable about overstaying his welcome. Before taking his leave Count Lajos thoughtfully presented him with a walking stick.

He picked one out of the stand and rather solemnly gave it to me. 'Here! A souvenir from Vesztö. My old shepherd used to make them, but he's dead now.' It was a very handsome stick, beautifully balanced and intricately carved all over with a pattern of leaves, and embowered in them, a little way down the shaft, were the arms of Hungary: the fesses on the dexter side were the country's rivers, while a triple hillock on the sinister, with a two-barred cross in the middle, symbolised the mountain ranges and the presiding faith, and over them both was the apostolic crown with its lop-sided cross. I was excited by such a present.

Count Engelbert von Wenckheim

With this kind gesture accepted, he decided to make his way to the next Wenckheim estate, which was owned by Count László Ernst Maria von Wenckheim at Doboz. His grandmother was Friederike, Countess Radetzky von Radetz, the favourite daughter of Austria's illustrious Field Marshall. He was twenty years older than his cousin Lajos.

He received an effusive welcome from the Count and his English wife. He was married to an English actress called

Eleanor Elizabeth Wood who came from Wednesbury in the English Midlands. 'He was rubicund and dashing and she—as I had been told but had forgotten—was English, indeed from London, "as you can tell," she said cheerfully. She had been on the stage—"not in a very highbrow way, I believe," someone had said—as a dancer or a singer, and though she was no longer a sylph, one could see how pretty she must have been, and how nice she was. Both of them radiated kindness.'

The Wenckheims were alarmed to hear that he was actually proposing to walk across Transylvania. Hungarian irredentist convictions raised their head and not for the first time on this journey. They told him the place was a den of thieves and riddled with VD. The very mention of Rumania made them uneasy and they become quite irrational.

[S]uddenly my hostess ran upstairs and came down holding a neat leather container that looked just too big for a pack of cards. 'You must take care of yourself, dear,' she said. Gróf László nodded gravely. I wondered what it could contain. The thought flitted through my mind, but only for a wild second, that it might be some counter-charm to the insidious medical threat of those valleys. 'One comes across all sorts of rum people on tours! This was given me years and years ago by an admirer of mine,' she went on. 'It's no use to me now so do please take it.' When the leather flap came out of its slot, it revealed a minute automatic pistol that could be described as 'a lady's weapon'; the butt was plated with mother-of-pearl and there was a box of rounds of a very small bore. It was the kind of thing women on the stage whisk out of reticules when their honour is at stake. I was rather thrilled and very touched.

The Dowager Countess Wenkheim with her son Count László

László moved to the Argentine after the Soviet advance on Hungary and died in Buenos Aires in 1956. His wife survived him by ten years, dying in Bariloche in Patagonia. Their descendants still live there today.

Leigh Fermor was now about to encounter the last of the Wenckheim trio on the Puszta and to experience what it was like to be a guest in a household which had remained largely unchanged since the glory days of the old Hungarian nobility. He was on his way to an estate which had hosted the Emperor Franz Joseph and the Empress Sissy for hunting parties. He made his way to Békéscsaba, an ancient Hungarian settlement, which was his last port of call on the Puszta. This leg of the journey he made by hitching a lift from a group of jolly nuns in a pony and trap. They dropped him at the village of Ókigyós (today called Szabadkigyós

The Wenckheim House at Doboz

The Wenckheim House at Doboz today subsumed into the village school

after a Communist era renaming) and here he found the entrance gates to one of the grandest Wenckheim houses.

Once through the great gates, I was lost for a moment. A forest of huge exotic trees mingled with the oaks and the limes and the chestnuts. Magnolias and tulip trees were on the point of breaking open, the branches of biblical cedars swept in low fans, all of them ringing with the songs of thrushes and blackbirds and positively slumbrous with

The Wenckheim Castle at Ókigyós (entrance front)

the cooing of a thousand doves, and the house in the middle, when the trees fell back, looked more extraordinary with every step. It was a vast ochre-coloured pile, built, on the site of an older building perhaps, in the last decades of the nineteenth century.

This Wenckheim castle is a glorious piece of whimsical architecture designed by Miklós Ybl, whose myriad architectural credits include the Budapest Opera House and a considerable swathe of Pest. Here Leigh Fermor found 'pinnacles, pediments, baroque gables, ogees, lancets, mullions, steep slate roofs, towers with flags flying and flights of covered stairs ending in colonnades of flattened arches' all combining to form Ybl's great creation of the late 1870s.

Ybl, the architect of the castle, had given himself free rein with armorial detail. Heraldic beasts abounded, casques, crowns and mantelling ran riot and the family's emblazoned swords and eagles' wings were echoed on flags and bed-curtains and counterpanes. The spirits of Sir Walter Scott and Dante Gabriel Rossetti seemed to preside over the place and as I had been steeped in both of them from my earliest years, anything to do with castles, sieges, scutcheons, tournaments and crusades still quickened the pulse, so the corroborative detail of the castle was close to heart's desire.

It was built for the fabulously wealthy Countess Kriszti-na Wenckheim, who instructed her architect that nothing in this masterpiece of neo-Renaissance eclecticism should be properly uniform, yet it should be harmonious in de-

Krisztina Wenckheim in 1884

sign, and should have as many windows as there are days in a year, as many rooms as weeks, and as many entrances as seasons. In 1934 it was home to Count József Károly Ferenc Mária Wenckheim, known as 'Józsi' and his wife Denise who was also his first cousin.

Leigh Fermor had already met Józsi and Denise Wenckheim at a luncheon party in their Budapest House at 3 Mányoki út in Buda. As he ambled up the long avenue which led to the castle, Józsi Wenckheim spotted him and immediately invited him to take part in a game of bicycle polo.

> He waved a greeting and cried, 'You are just what we need! Come along!' I followed him and the others across the yard to a shed. 'Have you ever played bike-polo?' he asked, catching me by the elbow. I had played a version of it at school with walking sticks and a tennis-ball on the hard tennis-courts; it was thought rather disreputable. But here they had real polo-sticks cut down to the right size and a proper polo ball and the shed was full of battered but sturdy machines. Józsi was my captain, and a famous player of the real game called Bethlen had the rival team; two other guests and two footmen and a groom were the rest of the players. The game was quick, reckless and full of collisions, but there was nothing to match the joy of hitting the ball properly: it made a loud smack and gave one a tempting glimmer of what the real thing might be like. I couldn't make out why all shins weren't barked to the bone; nor why, as one of the goals backed on the house, none of the windows were broken. The other side won but we scored four goals.

This game has stood out in the memory of many readers of *Between the Woods and the Water* principally because it had only recently gained popularity at the time of this sporting

A game of Bicycle Polo in 1908

event at the Wenckheims. The game was invented in Ireland in 1891 and was first played in County Wicklow. The
first international game was played at Crystal Palace between Ireland and England in 1901 so it was still relative-
ly in its infancy when Leigh Fermor made his international debut at Ókigyós.

Back in his bedroom in the castle he found one of the po-
lo-playing footmen trying to unpack the traveller's few tat-
tered items of clothing from his rucksack. Downstairs after
dinner he encountered this footman again. This time

> [M]y footman friend approached Count Józsi carrying an
> amazing pipe with a cherry-wood stem over a yard long
> and an amber mouthpiece. The meerschaum bowl at the
> end was already alight, and, resting this comfortably on
> the crook of his ankle, the Count was soon embowered
> in smoke. Seeing that another guest and I were fascinat-
> ed by it, he called for two more of these calumets and a

Archduke Joseph with whom PLF dined

The Dining Room at the Wenckheims where PLF dined with an Archduke

few minutes later in they came, already glowing; before they were offered, the mouthpieces were dipped in water. The delicious smoke seemed the acme of oriental luxury, for these pipes were the direct and unique descendants of those long chibooks that all Levant travellers describe and all the old prints depict; the Turks of the Ottoman Empire used them as an alternative to the nargileh.

The next evening, after further exertions at bicycle polo, the family and Leigh Fermor dined with a Habsburg Archduke. Archduke Joseph August Viktor Klemens Maria of Austria, Prince of Hungary and Bohemia, was briefly the Palatine or King's representative in Hungary. He was the eldest son of Archduke Joseph Karl of Austria and a member of the family known as the 'Hungarian Habsburgs'. During the Great War he was very much liked by the Hungarian troops under his command. The Archduke Joseph diamond, a 76.02 carat colourless diamond with internally flawless clarity, is named after him and was once his property. It was sold at Sotheby's in 2012 for 21 million dollars.

There were further entertainments at the Wenckheims before he took his leave of them, including a picnic and walks on the estate. The park was laid out in the English style with a lake and an artificial island. For the children the Wenckheims built a full-scale 'doll's house' which resembled a peasant house with a porch. An 'animal house' was situated in the garden, in which three chimps lived. All of this was complemented by a two-metre-deep swimming pool, tennis courts, and even a runway for a private plane which whisked Leigh Fermor's hostess's sister away while he was there. 'My hostess's sister Cecile looked at her watch and cried out, "I'll be late for Budapest!" We accompanied her to a field where a small aeroplane was waiting;

Count Szigi Wenckheim on the day of his wedding to Countess
Antoinette Cziráky de Czirák et Dénesfalva in 1941.
He was killed in WWII in 1943, aged twenty-two

she climbed in and waved, the pilot swung the propeller,
the grass flattened like hair under a drier and they were
gone.' A large clearing for playing bicycle polo in front of
the private family chapel completed this earthly paradise.

Leigh Fermor got on well with Szigi, one of the Wenckheim's sons, who took him up the castle's tower to view the
estate. He was going on to Ampleforth in a few months and
he told him he thought it was a very good school and that the
monks umpired cricket matches with white coats over their
habits. Szigi became a fighter pilot in the Hungarian air force
in World War II, and on December 14, 1943, while on a re-
connaissance flight, the Soviets shot down his aircraft near
Zhytomyr in western Ukraine. He was twenty-two years old.

Life at the Wenckheim estate carried on as it had always done—taking into account land reforms—until the advance of the Soviet army through Hungary in 1944. Count Józsi and his family then left the castle to its fate in the hands of the advancing Soviets in August 1944. They wrecked the fine interiors and looted anything that was of value. The house later became an agricultural college. Today it stands

Count Józsi Wenckheim in the 1930s

empty and forlorn but one can still make out the shape of the grass court where that game of bicycle polo was played on a summer evening in 1934. The Count and his family fled first to Vienna and then on to Algiers, where he died in 1952. His countess died in Algiers five years later. Count Krisztián Tasziló Wenckheim, grandson of Count Józsi, who lives in Bonn, is the heir to the Wenckheim estate of Ókigyós, should it ever become subject to Hungarian inheritance laws.

Leigh Fermor was now set to cross the frontier into Rumania and had been advised that he must do so by train, so

The Wenckheim family crypt at Doboz

he made his way to Lökösháza, the last Hungarian station before the frontier. He mused while he did so on his good luck in encountering families like the Wenckheims. However, this musing was tinged with not a little contrition:

[A] hint of guilt, hung in the air: I had meant to live like a tramp or a pilgrim or a wandering scholar, sleeping in ditches and ricks and only consorting with birds of the same feather. But recently I had been strolling from castle to castle, sipping Tokay out of cut-glass goblets and smoking pipes a yard long with archdukes instead of halving gaspers with tramps. These deviations could hardly be condemned as climbing: this suggests the dignity of toil, and these unplanned changes of level had come about with the effortlessness of ballooning. The twinges weren't very severe. After all, in Aquitaine and Provence, wander-

ing scholars often hung about châteaux; and, I continued
to myself, a compensating swoop of social frogmanship
nearly always came to the rescue.

With this little bit of self-flagellation completed he boarded
the Budapest night train from Lökösháza and prepared to
cross into Rumania.

III

# The Banat

*It's rather sad to belong, as we do, to a lost generation. I'm sure in history the two wars will count as one war and that we shall be squashed out of it altogether, and people will forget that we ever existed. We might just as well never have lived at all, I do think it's a shame.*

Nancy Mitford, *The Pursuit of Love*

As he neared the Rumanian frontier on April 27, 1934, a terrible sense of fear gripped him. This was not occasioned by a sudden recollection of the dreadful things he had heard about Rumania from his Hungarian hosts but rather by the sudden realization that he was carrying a gun and several rounds of live ammunition in his rucksack. As the train chugged along in the moonlight he hid the gun in the lining of his greatcoat. To his intense relief on arrival his passport was stamped, with bored ease, by an official at Kürtös (Cur-

Lökösháza station. PLF's departure point for Rumania

tici) which today is still an important railway junction between Central Europe and the western part of Rumania and a major crossing point between Budapest and Bucharest.

That evening at Pânkota he stayed with Imre Engelhardt, a Hungarian of Swabian origin, one of many families who settled in the region in the time of Maria Theresa. He was the owner of the Apollo Cinema in the town. He may have come from a family of that name who were substantial landowners in the area. Pânkota is situated about thirty-five kilometres from the county capital, Arad. He has little to say of his host and no trace has emerged from my search for him or his cinema in present-day Pânkota. His name and his cinema are recorded at the back of the 'Green Diary'. Today the town is a centre of light industry and of wine growing, hosting the vineyards of Pâncota, Silindia and Mocrea. The area of the Banat is under the protection of Saint John of Nepomuk, patron saint of the Danube watermen, the sanctity of the confessional and the Banat's German ethnic 'Donauschwaben'. Leigh Fermor would have passed by many statues of this revered churchman at different points along the Danube's banks.

His next destination was the historic market town of Borosjenő (Ineu). It is from Borosjenő that Count István Tisza, one of Hungary's greatest Prime Ministers, took his title and at Borosjenő that the Hungarians rather pointedly made their final surrender to the Russians, not to the Habsburgs, after the Revolution of 1848. Here, on a market day, he met, quite by accident, his next aristocratic host. He had already met Baron Tibor Solymosy de Loós et Egervár in Budapest and received an invitation to stay at his estate. The fortuitous meeting on market day hastened his arrival at the Solymosy castle. '[S]uddenly, hobnobbing with some farmers under an acacia tree, one foot on the step of a smart trap

Kürtös (Curtici) railway station today

Pânkota (c. 1934)

with a grey pony swishing its tail, here he was: jolly, baronial, rubicund, Jäger-hatted and plumed, an ex-Horse Gun-
ner in the same troop as the other Tibor. His face lit in welcome and two plum brandies appeared on a tray as though
by magic, and when they were swallowed we bowled off to
the hills.'

He reached the house in the late afternoon, accompanied
by his host. What lay before him he described thus:

Borosjenő, early 1930s

[A] Palladian façade just as night was falling. Two herons rose as we approached; the shadows were full of the scent of lilac. Beyond the french windows, a coifed and barefoot maid with a spill was lighting lamps down a long room and, with each new pool of light, Biedermeier furniture took shape and chairs and sofas where only a few strands of the original fabric still lingered; there were faded plum-coloured curtains and a grand piano laden with framed photographs and old family albums with brass clasps; antlers branched, a stuffed lynx pricked its ears, ancestors with swords and furred tunics dimly postured. A white stove soared between bookcases, bear-skins spread underfoot: and, as at Kövecsespuszta, a sideboard carried an array of silver cigarette-cases with the arms and monograms of friends who had bestowed them for standing godfather or being best man at a wedding or second in a duel. There was a polished shellcase from some Silesian battle, a congeries of thimble-sized goblets, a scimitar with a turquoise-encrusted scabbard, folded newspapers— *Az Ujság* and *Pesti Hírlap* sent from Budapest, and the *Wiener Salonblatt*, an Austrian *Tatler* full of pictures of shooting parties, equestrian events and smart balls far away, posted from Vienna. Among the silver frames was a da-guerreotype of the Empress Elizabeth—Queen, rather, in this lost province of the former Kingdom—another of the Regent dressed as admiral of a vanished fleet, and a third of Archduke Otto in the pelts and the plumes of a Hungarian magnate. Red, green and blue, the squat volumes of the *Almanach de Gotha* were ready to pounce. A glittering folio volume, sumptuously bound in green leather, almost covered a small table and its name, *Az ember tragediája*, was embossed in gold: *The Tragedy of Man*, by Imre Madács. It is a long nineteenth-century dramatic poem of philosophic and contemplative temper, and no Hungarian house, even the least bookish—like English houses with the vellum-bound Omar Khayyám illustrated by Edmund Dulac—seemed complete without it. Finally, a rack in the corner was filled with long Turkish pipes. This catalogue of detail composes an archetype of which every other country-house I saw in Transylvania seemed to be a variation.

He choose this point in his journey to reflect on the condition of these Hungarian estates in their island isolation in Rumania.

Baron Tibor Solymosy's house near Borosjenő

Estates, much reduced, existed still, and at moments it almost seemed as though nothing had changed. Charm and douceur de vivre were still afloat among the faded decor indoors, and outside, everything conspired to delight. Islanded in the rustic Rumanian multitude, different in race and religion and with the phantoms of their lost ascendancy still about them, the prevailing atmosphere surrounding these kastély-dwellers conjured up that of the tumbling demesnes of the Anglo-Irish in Waterford or Galway, with all their sadness and their magic. Homesick for the past, seeing nobody but their own congeners on the neighbouring estates and the peasants who worked there, they lived in a backward-looking, a genealogical, almost a Confucian dream and many sentences ended in a sigh.

Tibor Solymosy was the son of a wealthy landowner, Baron Lajos Solymosy de Loós et Egervár. He struck Leigh Fermor as a happy-go-lucky, slightly eccentric man, at ease with himself and with the world. He had a Polish ex-mistress, Ria Bielek, in residence and she appears to still have been a major influence in the young Baron's life when the young traveller came to visit. She was soon to be a force in Leigh Fermor's life too, bombarding him with books in various languages. She appears to have been quite a bibliophile:

Ria had countless French books and I borrowed them freely. Tibor was no reader but his forerunners must have been, for the library was well stocked, chiefly with works in Hungarian and German. Abandoning hope with Magyar, I longed to plunge deeper in German and began by reading all the rhyming couplets under the marvellous drawings of Max und Moritz and Hans Huckebein in a large volume of Wilhelm Busch. Elated by this and aiming higher, I moved on to Thomas Mann's *Tod in Venedig* and made a slow start, looking up every other word and seeking Ria's help when I got stuck.

His stay at this rural idyll was punctuated by visits to neighbouring estates, walks, picnics and a hill-top feast, complete with a gypsy band.

A bonfire was lit: a carriage disgorged four Gypsies—a violin, a viola, a czimbalom and a double-bass—who assembled under a tree. The amber-coloured wine we drank as we leant on our elbows round the flames was pressed from grapes which had ripened on the very slopes that dropped away all round. The vine-dressers climbed up, forming an outer ring, and when we had run dry they fetched fresh supplies from their cottages, filling all glasses until a cockcrow from an invisible farmyard spread an infectious summons through the dark; other cocks awoke; then the end of the Great Plain glimmered into being underneath us and everything except the Gypsies began to grow pale. Their strings and their voices kept us company all the way downhill, then through the gates and along the grass path through the trees. Our footprints showed grey in the dew; and when we reached the pillars along the front of the house, the sound of startled nests and birds waking up and the flapping of a stork from the pediment showed it was too late to go to bed.

Here the chronology in *Between the Woods and the Water* appears to become a little confused. He writes of visiting an estate at Tövicsegháza with Tibor and names it as the home of 'Jaas and Clara [Klára?] Jelinsky'. Jass, someone told, him came from 'an excellent family in southern Poland, eight thousand acres, not far from Cracow. His great-grandfather was Austrian Ambassador to Saint Petersburg and their Turk's head crest was granted after capturing three Tatar standards in the Ukraine.' In fact no land is registered in the region to anyone named 'Jelinsky' at this time. His wife Clara, he was told, was from 'an old, old, old, uralte'—here the speaker's eyelids would almost close as though in a dream at the thought of such antiquity—'family in the High Tatra mountains. They live in one of the most ancient castles in Hungary—Slovakia now, more's the pity! Counts since the reign of King Mátyás'. The only Transylvanian family of Polish origin with a similar name is that of Count Róbert Zselénszky, who held lands in the area around Arad, was a significant political figure and chairman of the Nemzeti Casino in Budapest—the Budapest gentleman's club to which the Hungarian nobility traditionally belonged. Leigh Fermor was taken to lunch at the club by Count Ladomér Zichy, who later tried to extricate Hungary from the Axis side towards the end of the war. It was as a result of Zichy's efforts that Admiral Horthy sent a delegation to Moscow to try and make agreement with the Soviets in the autumn of 1944.

Leigh Fermor describes 'Jaas and Clara Jelinsky' so clearly that one can only assume he is transposing them from another part of his journey. Can it be Count Róbert Zselénszky's family he is writing of? But Count Róbert did not have a son. He writes years after his visit of the 'low, ranch-like manor house of Tövicsegháza, for which I've searched the map in vain'. The reason the search possibly proved unfruitful is that the hamlet named properly Tövisegyháza, was by then renamed Zimandu Nou. There is a Countess Clara Zelensky listed in the addresses at the back of the 'Green Diary'. At this remove perhaps we shall never know the full answer. But the most likely answer is that

The Zselenszky house at Tövisegyháza

he met a descendant of Francis Zelenka-Zelinski who was made a count of the Kingdom of Galicia by Emperor Francis II in 1801. Francis' son, László, moved south to Hungary and married a wealthy heiress, Amalia Lovasz de Oettvenes, thus becoming owner of an estate in Uj-Arad and a house in Temesujfalu. His son, Róbert, was the first to use the name Zselénszky in its Hungarian form. In 1899, Emperor Francis Joseph I granted him an additional title of count—this time of the Kingdom of Hungary. He was married to Countess Klára Károlyi, which added greatly to his prestige and wealth. Since the Zselénszky house at Temesujfalu lay on the Rumanian side of the border after 1920, it is most likely that Jass was a kinsman of Count Róbert's. A possible source of this instance of confusion may be the simple mix-up over place names and the fact that he was relying largely on his memory of places he visited fifty years earlier. The Zselénszky house no longer stands today.

Before taking his leave of the Solymosy residence he made a visit to Arad. This town was ceded to Rumania in 1920 but remains a sacred place for Hungarians. It was one of the last places where the rebels of 1848 held out against the Habsburg forces and the place where thirteen Hungarian generals, some of whose families were intermarried with Leigh Fermor's hosts, were executed on October 6, 1849. These men are known as the 'Thirteen Martyrs of Arad'. Since their blood was shed there, Arad is considered to be the 'Hungarian Golgotha.' Because the executing Austrian officers clinked beer glasses as each Hungarian general met his fate, Hungarians resolved not to clink beer glasses for 150 years after the event. Many in Hungary still continue the tradition today even though the time frame of the vow has now lapsed.

While on their visit to Arad, Leigh Fermor and Tibor had an amorous encounter with two local girls—disproving, at least for this part of his life, Somerset Maugham's description of him in later life as 'a middle-class gigolo for upper-class women'. Maugham too was an old boy of the King's School, Canterbury, and like Leigh Fermor left the school at the age of sixteen. They did not find common cause in their shared English public school background when they met in 1956 at Maugham's villa in the South of France. Indeed, it was the very reason for the elder man's departure from the school which hastened Leigh Fermor's departure from La Mauresque, when, at dinner, he inadvertently imitated a man with a stammer. Maugham, who had an occasional pronounced stammer, was furious and asked him to leave the next morning.

Leigh Fermor made a sketch of the girl he met at Arad, whom he names as Izabella or 'Iza. '[S]he had very fair hair and dark blue eyes and spoke no word of anything but Hungarian, but this didn't matter at all. I wonder if her extreme fairness came from a dash of Slovak blood.'

The next family to give him refuge were Magyarized Swabians who had settled in Transylvania in lands regained

PLF's sketch of 'Iza' from Arad

after the defeat of the Turks. This ethnic group had been in Transylvania from the 18th century onward. It was the Saxons, and not the Swabians, however, who together with with the Hungarian Transylvanian nobility and the Szeklers, formed what was known as the Union of Three Nations, an

Arad, where PLF had a romantic tryst with 'Iza'

agreement signed in the fifteenth century, which effectively excluded the largely Rumanian peasantry from political influence. Leigh Fermor describes this wave of immigration thus: '[S]trangers were summoned from abroad; during the last three centuries the Holy Roman Empire and the Kingdom of Hungary became cosmopolitan, and in nothing so much as in the commanders of their armies; but their offspring had been assimilated long ago.'

Among these assimilated Germans was the family of János von Kintzig de Nyék, Leigh Fermor's host at a peculiar-looking house which resembled a French chateau in miniature. It was situated near the village of Tövisegyháza. It is not an ancient settlement, having its origins in a migration of Hungarian farmers to the area in the mid-nineteenth century. They came originally from northern Hungary, and were principally interested in the cultivation of the tobacco plant. A local landlord, Count Peter Csernovits—whose kinswoman Xenia Csernovits, as we shall see later in this narrative, became Leigh Fermor's lover in Transylvania—lost an estate in the area in a game of cards.

János von Kintzig was sixty-four when he hosted Leigh Fermor at his house. With his wife, Erzsébet (née Beliczay de Jeskofalva et Bajcza), he had two children, a son János who was in South America during Leigh Fermor's visit, and a daughter, Georgette, then aged thirty-one, and a famous equestrian champion. Georgette, whose English good looks impressed Leigh Fermor, was married to a Czech aristocrat, Károly Woracziczky de Pabienicz, whom she was seeking to leave at the time through a marriage annulment.

While staying at the von Kintzig's, Leigh Fermor again socialized with some of the grandest families in the land, including Princess Eugenie Odescalchi de Szerém, whom he describes as 'a tall princess, married to an erudite naturalist landowner called Béla Lipthay, from Lovrin in the Banat, was a descendant (not direct, I hope) of Pope Innocent IX of the famous house of Odescalchi, lords of Bracciano'. The Odescalchi Pope of whom he writes was not Innocent IX, but Innocent XI, known as 'the saviour of Hungary' for his efforts in financing the army in the war against the Turks. 'A man of total integrity and by far the greatest Pope of the seventeenth century' is how John Julius Norwich characterizes him in his history of the Papacy. A bronze statue of Innocent stands in Budapest's Vár just around the corner from the house where Leigh Fermor stayed. The Papal foot is represented, not crushing the usual symbolic head of the serpent, but instead the Turkish crescent. The statue of the Pontiff, a collaborative effort by sculptors József Damkó and Gyula Wälder, was unveiled in 1936. He was beatified by Pope Pius XII in 1956 after centuries-long oppo-

Pope Innocent XI 'saviour of Hungary' statue in Buda

sition from the French, who sought to deny Innocent any temporal authority in their lands. This led to a complete breakdown in relations between Louis XIV and the Pontiff. When Pope John Paul II required a final resting place within the Vatican, the remains of Pope Innocent XI, were moved to accommodate him, though this was not intended as a slight but more a matter of Papal housekeeping. A deliberate slight was visited on the late Pontiff by the Communist authorities in Budapest when they changed the name of Ince pápa tér to Hess András tér. This is the site where the statue of the Pope still stands. During the Antall government of the early 1990s when many street names in Budapest were reverting to their pre-war designation, a committee was set up to decide about the square in front of the Hilton Hotel. The vote was nineteen to stay the same and one to change back. The reason—'We don't want to celebrate foreigners'. So the 'saviour of Hungary' was usurped by a German printer named Andreas Hess. Gloria von Berg recalled that as a child when taking the bus down to Moszkva tér (today reverted to Széll Kálmán tér) when passing the statue the conductress used to proclaim loudly 'Hess papa tér!' A descendant of the seventeenth-century Pontiff, Carlo Odescalchi, became a Cardinal in the nineteenth century and it was he who was instrumental in giving to the Very Reverend Father Spratt, Master of Sacred Theology to the Carmelite Order in Dublin, the partial remains of the patron saint of lovers. On December 27, 1835, the cardinal sent the bones of St Valentine to Ireland. The saint's bones still rest in the Carmelite Church at White Friar Street Dublin, accompanied by a letter from Cardinal Odescalchi.

Eugenie Odescalchi came from the Hungarian branch of the Italian princely family of Odescalchi, which traces its roots back to the thirteenth century. Out of gratitude for the spiritual and financial aid received from the Odescalchi Pope in the campaign against the Turks, Emperor Leopold I raised the Pope's nephew, Livio Odescalchi, to the rank of a prince of the Holy Roman Empire in 1697. At the same time, in his capacity as King of Hungary, Leopold I granted the Odescalchi family a large part of the Szerémség—Syrmien in German—in eastern Slavonia, with the title, Duke of Szerém—'Dux Sirmiensis'.

The capital of the Odescalchi dukedom was the small town of Ujlak, better known today by its Croatian name of Ilok. It lies practically on the border between Croatia and Serbia. During the late Middle Ages, Ujlak was one of the largest towns in the Kingdom of Hungary with over 10,000 inhabitants. Its formidable castle was the property of one of the most powerful magnate families in medieval Hungary: the Ujlaki, as they were to call themselves, descended from Konth, Palatine of Hungary, who was granted the town and vast properties around it by King Louis the Great. Perhaps the most famous Ujlaki was Miklós (1410–1477) who was successively Ban of Macso, Vajda of Transylvania and King of Bosnia. The last member of this branch of the Ujlaki family was his son, Lőrincz (1459–1524), Ban of Macso and Prince of Bosnia. The Odescalchis restored the remains of Ujlak's medieval fortifications and built a new baroque residence, which they owned until 1944. The Odescalchi estates were in the former Upper Hungary near Nitra now in western Slovakia.

The family's great wealth passed in the female line on the death of the male head of the family, Benedetto Odescalchi, Pope Innocent XI, in 1689. A descendent of his, Prince Livio Odescalchi, who held a senior post in the court of the Empress Maria Theresa, inherited the estates granted to the family in Hungary in the eighteenth century and married

Pastel portrait of Princess Eugenie Odescalchi

a wealthy Hungarian heiress. With this alliance began the Hungarian line of the Odescalchi family and they continued to hold a leading position in Hungarian society until the advent of Communism in 1948.

Eugenie Odescalchi's father, Prince Livio Odescalchi, had three children by his first marriage to Baroness Ilona Zeyk de Zeykfalva. Eugenie was the third and youngest child of that union. The second child, Károly or Carlo as he was known, married Countess Klára Andrássy de Csíkszentkirály et Krasznahorka, known as Kája to family and friends, the granddaughter of one of Hungary's greatest statesmen, Count Gyula Andrássy. During World War II the Odescalchis were firmly anti-Nazi. Though divorced in 1929, after only eight years of marriage, Carlo and Klára

Odescalchi were united stalwarts of anti-Nazi resistance after Hungary entered the war on the Axis side in 1941. Kája already had something of an adventurous spirit and was
politically inclined from a young age. Mark Odescalchi recalled that she 'was active in politics between the wars, covered the Spanish Civil War as a journalist, to the irritation
of my grandfather, who was worried about her safety, and
in the early 1920s she helped her stepfather in his legitimist
activities. Gyula Andrássy the younger [the last Hungarian
Foreign Minister] organised the return of former Emperor
Karl to Hungary in 1921, which, of course, failed, Andrássy
being briefly imprisoned by Horthy.' Carlo worked at the en-
gineering firm of Ganz in Budapest and when the Nazis insisted on the sacking of a Jewish engineer, a decorated veteran of the Great War, for allegedly insulting Germany, Carlo
Odescalchi defended the man and publically claimed that he
too was no supporter of Germany or her war. The German
occupation of Hungary in March 1944 found Carlo Odescalchi on a Nazi blacklist. He spent the remainder of the war
in hiding until he could make good his escape to England,
where he died in 1987. It also put his ex-wife, Klára, in considerable danger, as is indicated in Foreign Office records of
the time, where the British minister to Budapest records his
reasons for requesting her being granted urgent safe passage
out of Budapest. In it he describes how Princess Odescalchi
helped Polish and British interests and the considerable risk
she was in from the Gestapo if she had stayed in Budapest.
He states that as her liberty and possibly her life was in danger because of these activities his decision to help her escape
was based on political rather than humanitarian grounds.

Klára, together with her friend Countess Erzsébet
Szapáry, did sterling work for Polish refugees who came to
Hungary after the invasion of Poland in 1939. This work,

Princess Klára (Kája) Odescalchi, by her first cousin,
Count Gyula Batthyány

together with her friendship with the British representative in Budapest, Owen O'Malley, put her life in jeopardy
once the German influence had spread in Budapest. She
held soirées for anti-German and left-wing Hungarian writers and journalists in her Budapest home overlooking the
Chain Bridge, where she introduced O'Malley, an Anglo-
Irishman, to many Hungarian anti-fascists. In late March
1941 O'Malley got word that Princess Klára was in immi-
nent danger of being arrested and arranged an exit visa for
her to Dubrovnik, accompanied by a naval attaché, Captain
Larkin. From there she was to be transported by submarine
by the Royal Navy to Greece and then onward to London.
She was, however, the unfortunate victim, in April 1941, of
the only Italian bombing raid on the port of Dubrovnik
during the entire war. Secret documents meant for the Brit-

Princess Klára Odescalchi with her
son Pál in 1926

ish government were found in her luggage after she was killed. 'An elegant, clever woman', is how the writer Balázs Lengyel remembered her many years after her tragic death.

At the time of Princess Klára's death her son Pál was in his final year at a Catholic school in Budapest. He too was soon to distinguish himself in the resistance movement, risking his life by moving Jews to safe houses around Budapest and even blowing up German military vehicles when the opportunity presented itself. He was also vehemently anti-Communist and was imprisoned by the Soviets in a camp near Gödöllő, north-east of Budapest, where he very nearly died before eventually escaping to England.

His kinswoman, Princess Margit Odescalchi, known as 'the Red Princess', became a Communist during the years of the Horthy regime. This was not especially motivated by doctrinaire belief in Communist principles but by the anti-fascist beliefs she developed after her family had suffered terribly at the hands of the Nazis. She was jailed by the Germans and her life was saved only at the last minute by a former family retainer when a group of fascist Arrow Cross thugs were sent to kill her. She was honoured by the Communist government and given over 300 acres of her estate back when land reforms were introduced. She decided to distribute this land among the former tenants on her estate and become an ordinary factory worker. She became a full member of the Communist Party and was returned as a member of parliament. Her brother, Nicky Odescalchi, was a fighter pilot with the Hungarian Air Force during World War II, but during an attempt to join the Allied side he was captured by the Germans at Anzio and hanged. He went naked to the gallows and it took fifteen minutes for him to die. He had destroyed his clothing and identity papers to thwart the German's investigation of him. Mark Odescalchi recalls his kinswoman's complex reasons for her flirtation with Communism:

> Margit Odescalchi was anti-Nazi during the War. Her husband, Count Gyorgy Apponyi, openly so in Parliament for which he was incarcerated in Mauthausen. When her brother Niki, was apprehended trying to escape in a German fighter to the Allied lines she was arrested and taken to Debrecen along with Niki's wife and their mother. Margit was interrogated next to cells from which she heard the screams of the inmates. After some weeks she was transferred to house arrest, eventually to be released by the Soviets. The execution of her brother by the Arrow-Cross authorities and their treatment of her and her family encouraged Margit to take a manual job in a local factory.

The propaganda possibilities of this conversion was not lost on the Rákosi regime. Margit was transferred to the Protocol Section in the Foreign Ministry and from thence in 1948 to the legation in Washington as Counsellor. Eventually she was recalled to Budapest and put out to grass in the Vinicultural Institute where her enthusiasm for the regime waned. In the Uprising of 1956 she escaped with her daughter Evi to Austria.

The 'Red Princess' Margit Odescalchi with fellow factory workers

Eugenie Odescalchi, Leigh Fermor's introduction to this extraordinary family, was married to Baron Béla Lipthay de Kisfalud et Lubelle, who came from one of the oldest families in the Banat. He was an expert lepidopterist and naturalist and survived Communism by working in natural history museums, where his extraordinary knowledge found a useful place. When they met Leigh Fermor in 1934 they were living on a neighbouring estate to the von Kintzigs at Lovrin in the Banat.

The day of their visit to the house they were accompanied by two Pallavicini brothers. Leigh Fermor reflected

Baron Lipthay's house at Lovrin in the Banat (c. 1934)

on the ancestry of these young men: 'Were they descended from the margrave who murdered Cardinal Martinuzzi,
the saviour of Transylvania, half-Venetian himself? I had
just been reading about him, but didn't dare to ask.' He is
referring here to the complex relationship between Cardinal György Martinuzzi, King John of Hungary, Emperor
Ferdinand of Austria, and the Sublime Porte—a relationship so convoluted that it led to the Cardinal being stabbed
to death in December 1551. An Italian Pallavicini was involved in the plot which ended the Cardinal's life. The Pallavicinis, like the Odescalchis had Italian noble roots and
the Hungarian branches of both families were connected
by marriage.

The connection between Leigh Fermor and the Pallavicinis was made in Budapest were he was brought to meet
the Marquesa Theodora (known as Thyra in the family) Pallavicini at the family palace at 98 Andrássy út where her
family had an apartment. She was about six months older than Leigh Fermor and the daughter of the Marquess

György Pallavicini. He was a member of the Hungarian parliament for several terms between 1906 and 1935 and held ministerial office in the short-lived administration of Count Móric Esterházy at the time of the Great War. Their attempts at reform were thwarted by the more conservative István Tisza and the administration fell after a few short months though Pallavicini went on to have a long parliamentary career. He was vehemently anti-fascist as were his sons. He spoke in the Upper House against the introduction of many of the anti-Jewish laws.

Engraving showing the stabbing of Cardinal Martinuzzi

The Pallavicinis did not have an estate nearby, so the two brothers were staying with their kinsfolk, the Lipthays, at Lovrin. Though he does not give their ages, the young Pallavicinis were most likely György and Antal, two of the three sons of the Marquess György Pallavicini. The boys' mother was Countess Borbála Andrássy, the granddaughter of Count Gyula Andrássy. Her published diaries are a detailed and often harrowing chronicle of life in Hungary under Communism but they are also a testament to the triumph of human will in the face of adversity.

The eldest of the two Pallavicini brothers who visited the von Kintzig estate while Leigh Fermor was staying was György Junior who was just three years older than him. During World War II he joined the resistance movement

Thyra Pallavicini in the 1930s

against the German occupation of Hungary and after the end of the war immediately undertook efforts to make Otto von Habsburg King of Hungary. He formed part of a royalist circle led by Cardinal Mindszenty and in 1945 tried to establish contact with Crown Prince Otto with a view to his being placed on the throne. The post-war control of Hungary by Soviet forces put an end to such aspirations and saw György Pallavicini, arrested, interrogated and sent to a Siberian labour camp, where he died in 1948. His kinsman Mark Odescalchi says of him: 'György was incarcer-

The Marquess György Pallavicini

ated in Dachau on 19th December 1944 for anti-Nazi activities and assigned prisoner number 135811. He was released when Patton's Third Army freed the inmates in April 1945 and returned to Budapest. Within a few months the Soviets imprisoned him and sent him to the Lubjanka in Moscow, where he died in 1948. His legacy which should be guarded has sunk without trace.'

His younger brother Antal was aged twelve in 1934. He later trained as an army officer at Budapest's Ludovica Academy and by 1943 was a lieutenant in a tank division of the Hungarian army. By the time of the German occupation of Hungary in 1944 he was a leader of the anti-Nazi, anti-fascist

The entrance front of the von Kintzig House around the time of PLF's visit

The garden front of the von Kintzig House today

resistance movement. Following the arrest of the leaders of the movement at the end of 1944, Pallavicini was arrested and taken as a Soviet prisoner of war in Timişoara, Rumania. After the war ended he joined the Hungarian Communist Party and was decorated for his war service in 1948. In 1950, he became brigade commander in a tank regiment. By 1949 he had changed his name to the more proletarian sounding Pálinkás. Soon after the outbreak of the 1956 Revolution he became disillusioned with his army role and he made contact with some of the young revolutionaries. In October he organized the escort of the imprisoned Cardinal József Mindszenty to Budapest. He continued his support for the revolution by the distribution of arms to the revolutionaries. He was arrested on December 25, 1956. After his release he was arrested again. The court sentenced him to life imprisonment in September 1957 but two months later the judgement was altered to the death sentence. The sentence was carried out

The Marquis Antal Pallavicini (Pálinkás) with Cardinal József Mindszenty in 1956.

on the morning of December 10, 1957, in Budapest. He was buried in an unmarked grave. After the collapse of Communism in 1989 he was posthumously pardoned, raised to the rank of Colonel and buried in a grave of honour.

All of this was far distant from those halcyon days of 1934 at the von Kintzig estate. Leigh Fermor's remaining days there were spent in leisurely pursuits, including paper chases in the woods on the estate, picnics and dinners. All of this was punctuated by a visit from Ria, Tibor von Solymosy's former mistress, a visitation which, by his own account, appears to have delighted Leigh Fermor. After dinner one evening they let off fireworks which they found in a woodshed. It seem an appropriate end to his departure, which so concerned his hostess that 'full of misgivings, [the] kind-hearted parents, and especially [the] mother, took the hazards of my journey very seriously. A son of hers had been in Brazil for fifteen years and if I had let her, she would have stuffed the whole of his wardrobe in my rucksack.'

Curiously, he ends his account of his stay with the von Kintzigs with the story of a fire at the house some years after his departure, remarking that it was conflict and political change which consumed all the other houses in which he stayed: '[B]ut in this charming and cheerful household, the tragedy that smote in the middle of that grim time had nothing to do with conflict: a fire sprang up in the night and the whole family and the combustible manor house that contained it were turned to ashes.' This offers yet another conundrum in this tale because the von Kintzig's house still stands today and the son of the house, János, died in New York in 1961. Rather oddly, the von Kintzigs are the only family he stayed with on this leg of the journey who do not feature in the address list at the back of the 'Green Diary'.

Monastery of Maria Radna today guarded by a statue of
St John of Nepomuk protector of the Danube watermen

There was a brief, but only brief, respite from staying
with the Hungarian nobility when he left the von Kintzigs
behind him. On June 1 he reached the ancient monastic settlement of Maria Radna, a Franciscan foundation perched
on a precipice high above the banks of the Maros River in
western Rumania. There has been a religious foundation
here since the fourteenth century when Carol Robert of Anjou, King of Hungary, constructed a place of worship ded-
icated to his uncle, Saint Louis of Toulouse, also related to
Saint Margaret of Hungary.

He was greeted by the portly figure of Brother Peter.
He found the only language they had in common was Lat-

in, so in the manner of the wandering scholars of old he did his best, in his schoolboy Latin, to engage the holy man in conversation. 'FRATER Petre, possumusne kugli ludere post Vesperas?' 'Hodie non possumus, fili,' Brother Peter said. 'Tarde nimium est. Cras poterimus.' 'Quando? Qua hora?' 'Statim post Missam. Expecte me ad egressum ecclesiae.' And so on until Brother Peter set up a game of skittles which engaged their attention until the bell for vespers summoned his partner to higher things. He spent the night in the monastery experiencing for the first time the *magnum silentium* of monastic religious observance and enjoying its quiet discipline. The next morning he bade farewell to the monks of Maria Radna and partly following the course of the Maros—Transylvania's greatest river—he arrived at the castle of Solymos. This, however, was not a place where he was to receive hospitality but rather a physical landmark on his way to his next hospitable Hungarian house. The castle of Solymos was a fortification built by János Hunyadi.

Solymos, the castle of János Hunyadi

188

Execution of the leaders of the Transylvanian Peasant Revolt of 1784

It marked the way to the castle of Kálmán von Konopy, an eminent agriculturalist and researcher, who invented a particular strain of winter wheat for which he was ennobled as Baron von Konopy. The mansion was rebuilt about 1800 in the neoclassical style. An earlier house was destroyed in the peasant revolt of 1784 known by the names of the three leaders as the Uprising of Horea, Cloşca and Crişan. It spread across Transylvania and was ruthlessly put down by the Hungarians.

Leigh Fermor describes the von Konopy house at Odvos, about forty-seven kilometres from Arad, as having something of the rural deanery about it: 'It might have been a rural deanery, and Mr v. Konopy [in fact, Baron], with his mild manner and silvery hair, could easily have been a clergyman; there was a touch of Evensong about him.' He may have grown too accustomed to staying in very grand houses but there was nothing of 'the rural deanery' about the grand neoclassical mansion which he now approached on June 2. He was obviously disappointed that his two days

The von Konopy house near Odvos, which is now in a sad and rapidly decaying state

in this house lacked 'the recent ambience of antlers and hooves and Tibor's memories of champagne out of dancers' slippers'. His host was a scholarly man who had two Swedish wheat experts staying with him and the conversation was mainly about wheat growing as the three men examined the wheat samples which covered much of the drawing room furniture. There seemed no respite from all this talk of wheat 'as we strolled from specimen to specimen the differences between turgid ears and the common bearded kind; then we surveyed the Polish variety and appraised the spikelets and the awns, the median florets and the glumes'. Some relief came in the form of a reading aloud of *The Story of San Michele*, which had been popular in England a few years earlier and tells the story of the restoration by Swedish physician, Axel Munthe, of a house on Capri. Today the von Konopy house stands in a sad and rapidly encroaching state of disrepair but it is not yet beyond redemption,

The von Konopy interior today

if some interested party would come to its rescue. During the Communist period the house served as the venue for pioneer youth camps. After the end of Communism in 1989 the castle was returned to the von Konopy family but sadly it remains looking for a sympathetic owner with the resources to restore it.

After just two days with von Konopy he packed his rucksack and bade farewell to the wheat-loving enthusiasts and ambled along the north bank of the Maros in the direction of the castle of Kápolnás. This had nothing of the aspect of a 'rural deanery' about it. On the contrary, it was one of the grandest houses in the Banat. He explains the resettlement of the area and the varied ethnic origins of the settlers.

Although this region south of the river was Transylvanian in feeling, strictly speaking it was the north-easternmost corner of the old Banat of Temesvár, named after its capital—Timişoara in Rumanian—which lies to the west. Lost by Hungary to the advancing Turks in the sixteenth century and largely depopulated, it was reconquered by Prince Eugene and Count Pálffy two centuries later, and re-settled. The largest single element of the modern province was Rumanian, as it had been all along my itinerary, but it was said that the newcomers were of such varied origins that a chameleon placed on a coloured population-map of the Banat would explode.

Kápolnás (Căpâlnaş) is an ancient fourteenth-century settlement about eighty kilometres east of Arad. Its antiquity is attested to by the remains of early medieval fortifications in the locality. Leigh Fermor was impressed by the grandeur of the eclectic architectural style of the castle which bears the name of the settlement. The garden front is dominated by four vast Corinthian columns supporting a heavy dentil cornice. He approached its balustraded sweep of double-fronted steps from the long avenue, passing a circular inset of box hedging. What stood before him was an early work by the distinguished Viennese architect Otto Wagner. He was twenty-six when he took on the commission in 1867 for his clients Ecaterina and Mihai Mocioni (the name was Magyarized to Mocsonyi). The house was an unusual structure in many senses. It resembled nothing of the simplicity of the style of Secessionist architecture with which Wagner later established his reputation. It would also be something of a curiosity for observant Hungarians after 1920 because it was influenced by the design of the Petit Trianon at Versailles.

Family tradition has it that the first two Mocioni brothers who sought refuge in Hungary died in the battles of Zenta in 1697 and the liberation of Timisoara from the Turks in 1716. In the mid-eighteenth century, Constantine Mocioni, an Armenian Orthodox priest living in Macedonia, resettled in Hungary. He had five sons, all of whom were successful businessmen in Budapest. One son was more successful than the next in accumulating great fortunes. As was often the case in the days of the Habsburg empire, being in trade was no bar to advancement in the peerage and two of Constantine's sons, Andrei and Mihai, were raised to the rank of noblemen by Emperor Joseph II. These two brothers are the ancestors of the two branches of the family which are directly linked to the house in which Leigh Fermor was a guest. They were known as the Mocioni and de Foeni families. Mihai Mocioni married his de Foeni cousin, Ecaterina in 1836, thus uniting the wealth of two families. It was

Count Jenő Teleki de Szék

Ecaterina's father who purchased about 6,000 acres of land around Kápolnás in 1853 from the Counts Zichy. It was into this family, the Mocsonyi de Foen, which Leigh Fermor's host, Count Jenő Teleki de Szék, had married, making him master of Kápolnás.

Leigh Fermor was astute in observing that the Mocsonyi family were stalwart defenders of the rights of the Rumanian peasantry. They were also unwavering in their adherence to their Orthodox faith while easily assimilating their Magyarization and remaining advocates of Rumanian culture in the Banat. This was what he especially noticed about the wife of his host, Katalin, known as Tinka in the family and to him as Catherine. 'Countess Catherine [...] was tall, dark-haired, fine-looking, very kind and very intelligent, and widely read in quite different fields from his.' In one particular, she was literally unique in this marooned Hungarian society: she was Rumanian; but of an unusual kind. Even today there is great respect for her family in the region.

PLF's pencil sketch of Countess 'Tinka' Teleki (June 1934)

Countess Tinka Teleki (c. 1934)

A number of Hungarian families in Transylvania had, in fact—however fervently Hungarian they became when they rose in the world—once been of Rumanian stock. The Countess's ancestors were from exactly this mould, except that, though they were Hungarian nobles, they remembered their origins and supported Rumanian aspirations. Magyar may have been their earliest language for generations; but, as MPs, they always expressed heterodox views in the Budapest parliament. Count Jenő, scion of one of the great Hungarian noble houses of Transylvania, was as deeply rooted in post-war resentment as any backwoods squire, though he was not emphatic in expressing it; while Countess Tinka, when occasion arose, was discreetly eloquent on the opposite side; and when one of them uttered controversial views, the other would later make it privately clear to a guest that they were nonsense. ('What a pity! Jenő's such a clever man, but so biased,' and, 'Well, I'm afraid Tinka was talking through her hat again.')

Countess Katalin's father Gheorghe Mocsonyi de Foen was born in 1823 in Budapest. He attended the law faculty of the university and after graduating he took over the management of the family estates at Vlajkovac and Birchiş. In 1859, Gheorghe married Countess Katalin's mother, Ilona Somogyi de Gyöngyös, whom Leigh Fermor encounters on his journey. In 1865, he was a Rumanian nationalist candidate, winning a seat in the Hungarian Diet, where, between 1865 and 1869 his speeches show him to be a stout defender of both the Rumanian and Serbian minority interests. He continued to win seats at all subsequent elections until 1875 despite the Hungarian government's best efforts to stymie nationalist aspirations by labelling them, among other

Gheorghe Mocsonyi de Foen

Vlajkovac castle, family home of Countess Katalin 'Tinka' Teleki de Szék

Vlajkovac castle today—a near ruin

things, 'Mocsonyism'. His constant generosity towards his Rumanian constituents made him and his family much beloved of the Rumanian people.

Leigh Fermor was extremely fortunate to see at such close quarters, and in such a civilized house, the tenets of the age-old Hungarian/Rumanian divide and we can be in no doubt but it helped him form his own views on the issue. They were, quite simply, that he liked the Hungarians and the Rumanians equally, if perhaps, leaning slightly towards the Rumanian nobility, whom he saw as more sophisticated than his Hungarian hosts in dress and reading tastes. This is certainly the view presented in the posthumously published *The Broken Road*, the last volume of the trilogy. He was, in many ways, the perfect guest, refusing to take sides in the internecine family quarrels thrown up by these social situations, in which he sometimes found himself, and resolutely refused to be drawn in as a referee. 'I am the only person I know,' he writes in *Between the Woods and the Water*, 'who has feelings of equal warmth for both these embattled claimants and I wish with fervour they could become friends. [...] My unsatisfactory position between the two makes me useless to both.' In the Teleki household such disagreements were frequent but always good-natured, and he recalls Count Teleki offering this view of his Rumanian neighbours: 'They seem to think the Treaty of Trianon awarded them Hungarian history as well as territory,' he said, moodily uncorking a bottle. 'It's like Corsicans celebrating Napoleon without mentioning France.' Leigh Fermor gives a brilliant analysis of the rivalries between the Hungarians and the Rumanians, greatly aided by his friendship with Rudi Fischer in Budapest, who was a relentless correspondent on this and other matters (there are over 400 letters from Fischer to Leigh Fermor in the PLF archive in Edinburgh). Perhaps Leigh Fermor took Bram Stoker's view about Transylvania as espoused by Count Dracula to the guileless Jonathan Harper:

We are in Transylvania, and Transylvania is not England. Our ways are not your ways, and there shall be to you many strange things. [...] For it was the ground fought over for centuries by the Wallachian, the Saxon, and the

Turk. Why, there is hardly a foot of soil in all this region that has not been enriched by the blood of men, patriots or invaders. In the old days there were stirring times, when the Austrian and the Hungarian came up in hordes, and the patriots went out to meet them, men and women, the aged and the children too, and waited their coming on the rocks above the passes, that they might sweep destruction on them.

His stay at Kápolnás was one of the longer of his sojourns in the Banat. Pál Teleki had written ahead from Budapest to his first cousin, Jenő, to give him advance notice of Leigh Fermor's arrival. He found Jenő Teleki and his Countess engaging company from the outset and it seems to have been entirely mutual. What he was unaware of when he first arrived, was that the pall of death hung over the house, be-

Otto Wagner's Kápolnás Castle, home of Count Jenő Teleki de Szék.
Today it is a psychiatric home

cause Countess Tinka's mother lay dying upstairs. *Noblesse oblige* or some such code prevented the Telekis from mentioning this or letting it interfere with their young guest's stay in any way. They entertained him as though there was nothing awry in the household.

'It's only early nineteenth-century,' the Count said, referring to his house, 'and perhaps a bit showy,' was how he modestly introduced Otto Wagner's early masterpiece to Leigh Fermor soon after his arrival at Kápolnás. He had greeted him on the terrace with the most unusual welcome delivered in a broad Scottish accent: 'Come and sit ye doon' was how this dapper Hungarian nobleman addressed his guest. That and many other Scots phrases peppered the Count's speech because he was raised by a nanny from the Highlands of Scotland. Teleki's reference to the late date of the house was, perhaps, a form of slightly inverted snobbery because the Telekis were an old family and the house was built by his wife's relatives, who were of more recent vintage.

Leigh Fermor had been aware since Budapest of the lineage of the Teleki de Szék.

His family had always been immersed in travel and science and literature. One branch explored Central Africa and discovered lakes and volcanoes on the Ethiopian border; my Budapest friend had mapped archipelagos in the Far East; Count Samuel Teleki, a wily Transylvanian chancellor in the eighteenth century gathered 40,000 books together in Márosvásarhély—Tárgu Mures, in Rumanian—in a library specially built for them, and gave it to the town: it was crammed with incunabula and princeps editions and manuscripts, including one of the earliest of Tacitus. (He must be the same as a namesake who collected and edited the epigrams of Pannonius.) A Count

Joseph Teleki, travelling in France with this bibliophile cousin, became a friend and partisan of Rousseau and launched a clever attack on Voltaire.

The Teleki Library survived the vicissitudes of Communism and even the scientific scholarly delusions of Elena Ceauşescu. The library contained many rare works on science, which fortunately escaped the attention of the 'Mother of the Nation' and dubious expert on polymer chemistry, who left school at the age of fourteen with a pass in needlework. Under Communism the Telekis themselves would

Count Samuel Tekeki wearing the robes
of the Order of Saint Stephen

not be as fortunate as their ancestors' books were. Cousins of Pál Teleki were relocated from a castle to a converted cow barn with no running water. His cousin Countess Ilona Teleki's mother took in laundry to make ends meet. Ilona became a factory worker and her brother a farm labourer. These were the branch of the Teleki family forced by circumstances to sleep in the cupboard of the public library founded by their ancestor. Later as, Ilona De Vito di Porriasa, Ilona Teleki became a successful Wall Street analyst. Her colleagues at work knew nothing of her aristocratic past. She would say to her family, when telling stories of her youth, 'but that's ancient history. We never need to talk about that anymore.'

Countess Ilona Teleki from castle to cow barn

Like his ancestor, Jenő Teleki was a great bibliophile and
he had a superb library at Kápolnás. It was in a vast room
centrally positioned in the house. Here Leigh Fermor spent
many happy hours reading through volumes of Hungarian
history and European fiction. He recalled years later that
the books even spilled over into his bedroom. In what was
a brilliant exercise in recall, he was able to detail, *memorit-
er*, much of what he saw and read in those extended warm
June summer days at Kápolnás.

> Henty, Ballantyne, *Jock of the Bushveld*, *Owd Bob*, *The Sto-
> ry of the Red Deer*, *Black Beauty*, *The Jungle Books* and the
> *Just So Stories*. There were any amount of Tauchnitz edi-
> tions, industriously tunnelled by insects, faded by the last
> summers of the Habsburg monarchy and redolent of those
> peaceful times when, apart from the habitual ragged fusil-
> lade in the Balkans, scarcely a shot was fired between the
> battle of Sedan and Sarajevo: Ouida, Mrs Belloc Lowndes,
> *The Dolly Dialogues*, *My Friend Prospero*, *The Cardinal's Snuff-
> box*, *The Indiscretions of Ambrosine*, *Elizabeth and Her German
> Garden*, Maupassant, Gyp, Paul de Kock, Victor Margue-
> ritte, early Colette.

But the most important and revealing trove was half a doz-
en historical novels by the Hungarian writer Mór Jókai
(1825–1904), translated in Victorian days:

> *Midst the Wild Carpathians*, *Slaves of the Padishah*, *An Hun-
> garian Nabob*, *The Nameless Castle*, *The Poor Plutocrats*, *Pretty
> Michael*, *Halil the Pedlar*, *Ein Fürstensohn*—there were sever-
> al more. The plots were laid in stirring times: the Kossuth
> rebellion, the wars against the Turks with the whole of
> Transylvania going up in flames; soaring castles, yawning
> chasms, wolves, feuding magnates, janissaries, spahis, pa-

The chipped and faded splendour of Kápolnás - today a psychiatric home

shas with six horsetails, sieges, battle-fields and last stands; stories involving all the great figures of local history: Hunyadi, Zrinyi, Thököly, the Rákóczi dynasty, Bocskays, Bethlens, Báthorys, Bánffys—B's seem to abound among Transylvanian leaders and princes; and Telekis, of course. The plots were a heady mixture of Scott, Harrison Ainsworth and Dumas père transposed to the Carpathians and the Puszta.

Leigh Fermor delighted in the Count's obtuse sense of scholarly abstraction. One day, sitting in the library, he asked his young guest what he thought the ancient Huns wore? When he answered 'animal skins' the Count shot back with 'so should I,' he said, 'but we are wrong,' and he read out from Ammianus Marcellinus' account of the mission to Attila: 'They are clad in linen raiment or in the skins of field mice sewn together.'

There were many diversions from scholarly pursuits while he was staying with the Telekis. Countess Tinka arranged a few motoring trips, usually with herself at the wheel. One such took them past the Hill of Déva whereon sits the imposing Castle of Déva. It was here that Prince Ákos Barcsay was ensconced with his fifteen-year-old bride, Ágnes Bánffy, in 1660 when he, Prince of Transylvania, then a mere fifty-one, became temporarily distracted from pressing affairs of state by the young temptress. Soon after, he was murdered by a crafty enemy, János Kemény, who took advantage of the Prince's amorous distractions and seized the princely title for himself.

Samuel Teleki's magnificent Library at Marosvásárhely (Târgu Mureş)

The castle is such an important part of Hungarian folk-loric tradition. 'The Ballad of Clement the Mason' tells of twelve stonemasons who are commissioned to build the fortress of Déva on a promontory outside the eponymous city but their failure to make progress with the task takes a sinister turn. They agree to perform a ritual sacrifice by killing the wife of the first mason who arrives with their daily food hamper. This ritual mixing of her blood with the mortar would then assure success. It is the wife of Clement, the master mason, who arrives first and is to be sacrificed. When he sees her carriage arriving along the road below the fortress he incants this prayer:

> My God, my God, take her away somewhere!
> May all my four bay horses break their legs,
> May all the four wheels of my coach break into pieces,
> May the burning arrow of God's thunderbolt fall on the road,
> May my horses rise up and turn home!

Déva received much-favoured status in the reign of János Hunyadi, the White Knight of Wallachia, ruler of Transylvania, that figure much beloved of Hungarians and Rumanians alike. He was, according to his seal of office, *'Ioanis de Huniad, Gubernatoris Regni Hungarie*—John Hunyadi, Governor of the Kingdom of Hungary, effectively the Regent during the minority of Ladislaus V. Hunyadi was, in 1453, the first in the land to receive a hereditary title being made *perpetuus comes* (perpetual count) and awarded the Saxon district of Beszterce (now Bistriţa in Rumania). The city of Déva became a centre of military and administrative authority under his rule. It was partially destroyed by the Turks, who had been kept at bay by Hunyadi, until things began to deteriorate, about sixty years after his death

Hunyadi in full battle cry

in 1456. His campaigns in the Balkans severely dented the power of the Sublime Porte in those parts and Hunyadi was a hero in Bosnia, Serbia, Bulgaria, Albania and Belgrade. The church bells of Christian Europe were rung at noon to celebrate Hunyadi's deliverance of it from the Turks. They are still rung at noon in Hungary today, where many a visitor mistakes them for the Angelus bells. Hungarian sayings still abound with references to battles lost and won. When something falls and breaks a Hungarian is quite likely to say in dismissal of the act, 'More was lost at Mohács.'

As Leigh Fermor motored beneath the fortress of Déva with the Telekis, his head was full of the brave and heroic deeds of Hunyadi, and of the deeds of Hunyadi's son, King Matthias Corvinus—progenitor of the eponymous library. It was in the reign of Matthias that some of Leigh Fermor's hosts received their titles of nobility, a fact he delighted in recording. By this stage of his journey he was becoming something of an amateur expert genealogist on matters relating to the Hungarian nobility. His hours spent reading in Count Teleki's library had barely prepared him for what he was now about to encounter on their road trip. Turning south at the Hill of Déva they drove on until before them in all its whimsical glory stood the castle of Vajdahunyad, Hunyadi's fantastical fortification. There are few times in *Between the Woods and the Water* or elsewhere in his writing when he entered such a rhapsodic state of fugue when describing a piece of architecture as he does when describing Vajdahunyad. This baroque concerto of language is one of the most exhilarating architectural descriptions in English travel literature; releasing in him at once the enthusiasm of the mature scholar and the exhilaration of the young man.

> [A] building so fantastic and theatrical that, at a first glance, it looked totally unreal. Like many castles, it had once been damaged by fire and built up again in its former shape; but it was perfectly genuine. The bridge led to a sallyport in a tall barbican which ended high above in a colonnade supporting a vertiginous roof that soared in a wedge, like the great barbicans in Prague: spikes of metal or shingle erected for the laming of infernal cavalry flying low after dark. Towers, clustering at different heights, some square and some round and all of them frilled with machicolations, were embedded in the steep fabric. The light showing between the pillars holding up the great angular cowl of the barbican gave the pile an airy, lifted, slightly improbable look, and the closely spaced parade of the perpendicular buttresses made the upward thrust still more impetuous. Beginning deep in the abyss, these piers of masonry ascended the curtain wall and the donjon and the outside of the banqueting hall in unbroken flight and then burst out high above in a row of half-salient and half-

engaged octagonal side-towers, all of them lighted by windows which carried on a dominating line of mullioned lancets, and an interweaving network of late gothic tracery branched and flourished and linked them together with all the impulse and elaboration of the French Flamboyant style. Along the eaves of the precipice of roof overhead, the jutting towers ended in disengaged extinguisher-tops, cones that alternated with faceted octagonal pyramids and barbed the eaves with a procession of spikes, while beyond them coloured tiles diapered the roofs in intricate patterns, like those on St Stephen's in Vienna. Beyond the sallyport, the inner courtyard mounted in galleries and balustrades and tiers of Romanesque arches; cusped ogees led to spiralling steps; and indoors, springing from the leafy cap-

Vajdahunyad the castle of János Hunyadi over which PLF rhapsodized.

itals of polygonal rose-coloured marble pillars, beautiful late gothic vaults closed over the Hall of the Knights.

They picnicked within the shadow of Hunyadi's castle, the Telekis exchanging good natured banter about how the Rumanians and the Hungarians each claimed Hunyadi as their own. This was prompted by Leigh Fermor mentioning that on the information boards within the castle, the

The Castle of Deva beneath which PLF picnicked with the Telekis

Rumanians made no mention of Hunyadi's Hungarian heritage. Perhaps the old warrior had wandered too far away from the arms of Eastern Orthodoxy for the comfort of the powers in Bucharest. Or perhaps Rumania herself, in the *interbellum* period, was moving too close to eventual fascism, jingoistic nationalism and the grip of the Iron Guard, to allow mention of Hungary in any public notices in historic sites. It was little different on the other side of the border to the west when it came to laying claim to Hunya-di heritage. These age-old enmities still find a stirring and sometimes provocative resonance, even today, in conversations to be had in both countries where these prejudices have an ancient and lengthy pedigree.

As the warm Transylvanian summer enticed the Tele-kis out of their house, they visited and were visited in return by, a succession of friends and relations, most of whom Leigh Fermor enjoyed considerable social interaction with. The expeditions 'warranted the emergence of the car, a solemn event in these regions of bad roads. The Countess drove, and when a wandering buffalo held us up, the Count, with memories of Cowes, would lift his hand and murmur, "Sail before steam!" and we would wait while it lumbered over.'One of the first excursions was to a luncheon party in a house then owned by a member of the Hunyadi family, who was not a direct descendant of Leigh Fermor's hero János Hunyadi. The house, a large neoclassical structure, was at Soborsin (Săvârşin), north of the Telekis' residence. The estate entered the Hunyadi family through a fortuitous marriage to the ancient noble family of Nádasdy. A Nádasdy married the notorious 'blood' Countess Elizabeth Báthory in the sixteenth century. Her notoriety, a blend of Transylvanian fact and fiction, extends to the myth of her bathing in the blood of virgins to preserve her youth. It is far more likely that her trial and incarceration were politically motivated events but this must be tempered by the fact that the Countess also appears to have had quite a sadistic streak. All splendid stuff, no doubt, for luncheon conversation.

Leigh Fermor's hosts at the luncheon party at Sobors-in were Count and Countess Ferenc Hunyady de Kéthely. His ancestor, András Hunyadi, was ennobled by King Ru-dolf of Hungary in 1607 and the family became counts of

the Holy Roman Empire in 1797. Another relative of his was
Princess Consort of Serbia, Júlia Hunyady de Kéthely, who
married King Mihailo Obrenović III of Serbia. After his assassination in 1868 she married Duke Karl von Arenberg,
Prince von Recklinghausen, making her, at various stages
in her life, a Countess, a Duchess and twice a Princess. Fe-

Soborsin Castle as PLF would have known it in 1934

renc Hunyadi's wife was born Countess Márta Lónyay, and
was from a family whose earliest records date to the eleventh century. Her mother was a Kendeffy, from one of the
most ancient Transylvanian noble families. 'A tall, distinguished couple' is how Leigh Fermor remembered the Hunyadis. It was through the marriage of the count's father,
Count Károly Hunyady de Kéthely, to Countess Maria-
Irma Nádasdy, that Soborsin Castle came to be a Hunyadi
property. It was inherited by Ferenc Hunyadi just one year
before Leigh Fermor visited.

Ferenc Hunyadi was a member of parliament and quite
politically active some years before Leigh Fermor met him,
but by the time of the luncheon party at Soborsin he had effectively retired temporarily from political life to concen-
trate on the management of his estates. Hunyadi had quite
a distinguished record during the First World War and spent
eighteen months as a prisoner of war in Rumania. He was

Count Ferenc Hunyadi as a young Hussar

the recipient of several military decorations and was made a *vitéz* (knight) by the Regent Horthy in the early 1920s. It was somewhat surprising that a member of the Catholic court aristocracy accepted an honour from the Regent because many among the Catholic nobility kept their distance from Horthy, especially during the early period of the Regency. But Hunyadi was perhaps somewhat less rigid in these matters than some older relatives of his might have been.

A legitimist by conviction, he entered parliament as a representative of the Christian Economic Party, an organization which he left three years later in 1930. He was elected once again, though with some difficulty and temporarily retired from politics. In 1937 he published a historical novel entitled *Szétesett ország* (A country fallen apart). It dealt with the period following the Hungarian defeat at Mohács in 1526 and received mediocre notices, some praising its 'historic' language but damning its outdated style.

After 1939 he joined Béla Imrédy's newly founded Magyar Élet Pártja (Party of Hungarian Life). This shows Hunyadi was by now straying far from conservative, legitimist and Catholic principles and making his way to the anti-Semitic far right. Imrédy established his party following his forced resignation as Prime Minister when it was discovered that though he introduced the second anti-Jewish law in parliament, he himself was of distant Jewish descent. Hunyadi was now associated with a party and with a man who was widely believed to be the foremost champion of German interests in Hungary. This explains the tone and content of his speech to the lower house of parliament on July 2, 1941.

Participating in the debate following the presentation by the government of the Third Jewish Law, Hunyadi said he agreed with its principal aim, that of making marriage between Jews and non-Jews illegal. He added that had a similar law been passed in 1867, many future problems could have been avoided. In his view, the introduction of civil marriage was the main culprit, for after this mixed marriages increased rapidly. Reflecting on the evil which results from marriages between Jews and non-Jews Hunyadi asks his fellow parliamentarians to cast their eyes back 'to 1918 and 1919 when the streets of Budapest in those years were dominated by roving terror detachments whose members combined Semitic looks with a Hungarian peasant boldness, with which they attacked the Hungarian nation and state. We have a clear illustration here of what happens when we permit Jewish capitalists to reproduce with simple girls of the proletariat or the peasantry.'

Hunyadi added that the law being debated did not go far enough. An additional law should be drawn up, 'as soon as possible' to outlaw all sexual relations between Jews and non-Jews as well. He then addressed the rather bizarre notion of Jews assuming the old historic noble names during the process of Magyarization. He told the house, 'Those who are Jews should be deprived of their [assumed] historic names' and 'I am particularly interested in this matter since I seem to have more Jewish relatives in name than anyone else.' Hunyadi seems to have rather conveniently forgotten that his own family changed their name from the rather undistinguished, Nagy, which in Hungarian means simply 'big', to the more aristocratic and historically grand name of Hunyadi. We have as the incontrovertible source of this information none other than a man called Ivan Nagy, the most distinguished Hungarian genealogist, who writes in his history of Hungarian family names: 'The original name of the Counts Hunyady de Kethely family was Nagy. The founder of the family, András Nagy, came from Hunyad in Transylvania and was an official in the service of László Majthényi, Provost of Buda and Bishop of Szerem. He was ennobled and granted arms by King Rudolph in 1607. Both he and his sons used the name Nagy which gradually became Nagy alias Hunyad and Nagy de Hunyad.' It puts one in mind of Oscar Wilde's great witticism about the aristocracy: 'You should study the Peerage. It is the one book a young man about town should know thoroughly, and it is the best thing in fiction the English have ever done.'

Liberal thinking Hungarians placed no restrictions on the choice of name those who wished to Magyarize their surnames might care to adopt. Historic family names as such were not protected by law until the interwar period when legislation protecting historic names *was* introduced. Hunyadi's mention of 'Jewish name relatives' probably refers to the writer Sándor Hunyadi, the illegitimate son of the novelist Sándor Bródy, who was of Jewish descent. In *Ulysses*, James Joyce names Leopold Bloom's Hungarian

James Joyce named Leopold Bloom's Hungarian Jewish
maternal grandfather 'Julius Karoly'.

Jewish maternal grandfather 'Julius Karoly'. While Karoly
is a name which occurs frequently in Hungary, the mere
addition by Joyce of an 'i'—for the Hungarian noble family
spells it 'Karolyi'—would have made the Blooms of Dublin
into suitable material for Count Ferenc Hunyadi's chagrin.

There is little evidence that Jews were more readily ap-
propriating historic names than anyone else. And when
they did, they seemed to have a penchant for old Transylvanian names. Sir Alexander Korda's family took the name of
the extinct Counts Korda, Béla Kun's name came from the
Counts Kun—who in the nineteenth century took to spell-
ing their name with a double 'u'—or the popular humor-
ist George Mikes who borrowed his name from the grand
Transylvanian family of the Counts Mikes.

The resurrection of Count Hunyadi's political career
came some years after Leigh Fermor's meeting him. The
house which they lunched in was sold ten years after Leigh
Fermor's visit to King Michael of Rumania. There was another smaller house at Lók, also known as Nagylók, in Fejér
County, which became his home after Sorborsin was sold to
the King in 1943. The King bought it as a gift for his moth-

King Michael I of Rumania bought Soborsin Castle in 1943

er, but the family had little time to enjoy it. Soborsin was confiscated by the Communist authorities in 1947 and became successively, a tuberculosis sanatorium, a mental institution and in 1967 was taken over by someone who unfortunately escaped incarceration there, Communist dictator Nicolae Ceaușescu, who made it one of his many residences. It was returned to the Rumanian Royal family after the collapse of Communism and is now open to the public on certain days of the year.

Back in that June day of 1934 Leigh Fermor remembered just one luncheon guest at Soborsin, whom he describes as 'a Hungarian diplomatist called Baron Apor. [...] [I]t is odd how figures seen only once suddenly shoot into the memory, complete at all points: he had a spherical, totally shaven head and I can see the shine of his scalp, and the veined bloodstone on his signet ring, as though he had left the

Soborsin Castle today, once again a Rumanian Royal residence.

room a minute ago; but can't recall a syllable that was said.'
Perhaps he had met too many Archdukes to be impressed
by a mere Baron, but there was nothing ordinary about this
Baron. His father was Baron Gábor Károly Vilmos Apor de
Altorja and his mother Countess Fidele Pálffy ab Erdőd,
who together raised a family, which left an extraordinary
mark on the map of Hungary's humanitarian landscape in
the mid-twentieth century. The were descended from one of
the oldest Transylvanian families.

By 1934 Baron Gábor Apor de Altorja had served in diplomatic posts in Berlin and Warsaw and returned to Hungary in 1927 to become head of the Political Department at the
Foreign Ministry, a post he still held when Leigh Fermor
met him. He was decidedly opposed to the extreme right-
wing policies of then Prime Minister Gömbös. He was later
Ambassador to the Holy See during the war years where he
exerted considerable influence on fellow Vatican diplomats
to help save Jewish victims of Nazism. His detestation of the
Nazis' influence over Hungary made him resign his post in

1944. He wholeheartedly supported Prime Minister Miklós Kállay's many overtures to the Allies, which proposed removing Hungary from the Axis side during the war.

Gábor Apor was also the brother of the martyred Bishop of Győr, Baron Vilmos Apor de Altorja, who was a fearless protester against the persecution of Hungarian Jews. On Whitsunday 1944 he preached against what was happening to the Jews of Győr: 'He who assumes that men, whether Negroes or Jews, may be tortured must be regarded as a pagan. [...] One cannot tolerate anti-semitism. It must be condemned from the Pope down to the least of the bishops. [...] One must state openly that nobody must be persecuted for the blood in his veins.' In 1944 he wrote to the Arrow Cross Interior Minister, Gábor Vajna, who was busy establishing the Budapest Ghetto and collaborating in the deportation of Budapest's Jews: 'As bishop of the an-

Baron Gábor Apor, Hungarian diplomat

Blessed Bishop Baron Vilmos Apor

cient city of Győr, I protest before God, Hungary and the world against these measures, which are in contradiction to human rights. I hold you responsible for all the cases of sickness, humiliation and death caused by these measures.' Despite his protests the Jews of Győr were rounded up and sent on cattle trucks to their death. On Good Friday, March 28, 1945, Bishop Apor was protecting a group of women who were hiding in his residence when Soviet soldiers entered and attempted to rape the women. Bishop Apor intervened but one of them turned his gun on him and shot him at close range. He died from his wounds a few days later. Only in 1986 did the Communist authorities allow his body to be entombed in the cathedral at Győr. He was beatified by Pope John Paul II in 1997. His brother Gábor died in Rome in 1966.

Leigh Fermor's hostess, Countess Irma Hunyadi, died in Budapest in 1948 before she could feel, as a 'class enemy', the full brunt of Communism. Count Ferenc was sent into internal exile, for four years from 1952, with a family of kulaks (affluent peasants) in Kőtelek in the Hungarian Great Plain. Later he lived at different Budapest addresses. He regularly and pointlessly petitioned the Budapest Museum authorities for the return of some of the family treasures which were plundered from his houses. He married, secondly, Aranka Machacek from Kassa, who was nearly twenty years his junior, and endured the rigors of life in Communist Hungary until his death in Budapest in 1966.

An interesting historical sidebar to the impeccable antifascist credentials of the two extraordinary Apor men, one of whom Leigh Fermor met at the Hunyadis', was an aristocratic relative on their mother's side whose moral compass was very much off-course from theirs. He was of quite the opposite political hue and held extreme fascist views. Count Fidél Pálffy was a staunch supporter of the Nazi ideology in Hungary—so much so that he was considered by some in the SS in Berlin to be suitable leadership material to rule Hungary in the period of Nazi dominance in the country. After the war, the People's Tribunal found him guilty of collaboration and he was hanged for treason in March 1946. There was much controversy surrounding the decision to hang him because it was claimed that other than his pro-Nazi writings and his membership in Szálasi's fascist government as Agriculture Minister, there was little evidence of any actual war crimes other than the obvious one of willing collaboration. Pálffy was one of the first members of Szálasi's Arrow Cross government to face trial. It was felt that the Communists wanted to make an example of someone from an old aristocratic family in an attempt to show that *all* aristocrats were corrupt fascists. Others felt a very lengthy jail sentence would have been more appropriate and that there were bigger fish who had escaped the net. The real problem with Pálffy was that as well as his detestable politics, he was weak of character. Financial pressure—he was bankrupt by the early 1930s— drove him into the arms of National Socialism in the naive belief that the new order would bring with it a new prosperity. There were many aristocrats in similar financial circumstances who acted more honourably. Fidél Pálffy's brother Géza was one such. He was staunchly anti-Nazi and played an active part in the Resistance in Hungary. He tragically met his end in a Soviet Gulag in the early 1950s.

Another fellow aristocrat, from a similar background to Pálffy, who also supported the fascist Arrow Cross regime was Baron Dr Gábor Kemény. Kemény was a youthful thirty-four when he became Foreign Minister in Szálasi's government. He came from a Transylvanian noble family, which included among its number János Kemény, who had

Arrow Cross Foreign Minister Baron Gábor Kemény being arrested in 1945

been Prince of Transylvania in 1661. The Baron's wife (née Elizabeth Maria von Fuchs) was said to be of Jewish descent, something she denied after the war, when she also defended her husband's reputation, claiming he 'helped save many Jews, and that the unjust idea of collective guilt led to his arrest, condemnation, and execution'.

Elizabeth Kemény herself supported at least some of Raoul Wallenberg's efforts to save Hungarian lives. It was even suggested by some in Budapest that the beautiful baroness was Wallenberg's mistress, something she also denied in her post-war testimony. She was pregnant with Kemény's child when she convinced her husband to validate Wallenberg's Swedish passports for Hungarian Jews when Szálasi had declared them invalid. Kemény's most foolhardy act was to try, with relentless naivety, to gain legitimacy abroad for the Szálasi regime at a time when Hungarian ambassadors in several diplomatic missions, including the Turkish capital Ankara, refused to recognize it and remained *en post* and loyal to the Horthy administration. By the time Budapest had fallen to the Allies in February 1945, Kemény had already left the city but was later captured and arrested. At his trial by the People's Tribunal he was sentenced to death for war crimes and high treason. He was hanged in Budapest in March 1946.

Among the princely houses of Hungary there was a member of only one such family who espoused Nazi principles from the time of Hitler's assuming power in Germany. Count Sándor Festetics had served in Mihály Károlyi's cabinet as Minister for Defence in 1918. He was never totally estranged from parliamentary politics but like Pálffy become convinced of the merits of Nazism around the time Leigh Fermor arrived in Budapest. Despite putting the considerable fortune he had inherited from his uncle Prince Tasziló

Festetics at the disposal of a nascent Hungarian Nazi party in 1933, he found himself expelled from the Hungarian Socialist People's Party because it was felt his commitment to anti-Semitism lacked the fervour of a true believer and he continued to give employment to Jews on his estates.

Of lesser social rank than Sándor Festetics but of more fervent commitment to the doctrine of Nazism was Zoltán Böszörmény, who came from a bankrupt family of minor Hungarian landed gentry and had been on the fringes of Béla Kun's regime in 1919. He was active in Budapest during the time of Leigh Fermor's stay. After a meeting with Hitler in 1931 he became enamoured of the more hard-line elements of Nazi beliefs and founded the National Socialist Party of Work, which adopted the swastika as its emblem and a verbatim adoption of Hitler's National Socialist programme. Having modestly declared himself 'a giant intellect and a great Hungarian poet with a prophetic mission', he proceeded to lead an attempted coup on Budapest on May Day 1936 but his raggle-taggle group of supporters were quickly suppressed and Böszörmény, who pleaded insanity at his subsequent trial, escaped to Germany from where he failed in a petition to Communist hardliner Mátyás Rákosi in 1948 to be allowed to return to Hungary. Such were the stirring times and circles in which Leigh Fermor was vicariously moving in 1934.

Leigh Fermor's next encounter with the nobility came in the form of a visiting house party from Bulci (Bulch) Castle, which lay a few kilometres west of Soborsin. The house was owned by a cousin of his hostess, Tinka Teleki. Rather oddly, Leigh Fermor describes the master of Bulci in great physical detail but does not name him. Nor does he make it exactly clear if he ever actually visited Bulci apart from saying there was 'daily to-and-fro movement' between the two castles, especially while the house party, which mainly con-

Baron Antoniu Marius Mocsonyi de Foen

sisted of guests from Bucharest, was staying at Bulci. But the generous nature of his hosts makes it unlikely that he was excluded from these visits. The master of Bulci he described as having a high-bridged nose and receding chin, fiftyish, cosmopolitan, urbane, clever and an excellent shot, was Baron Antoniu Marius Mocsonyi de Foen, member of parliament, government minister and Grand Master of the Hunt of the Royal House of Rumania.

During his tenure Bulci was a centre of royal entertainment with frequent visits by King Carol II, the controversial 'playboy king', as he was known. Carol, having ousted his son King Michael I in a coup, was King of Rumania again by the time Leigh Fermor encountered his Master of the Royal Hunt at the Teleki house at Kápolnás.

Among the guests from Bulci was 'a tall diplomatist with a monocle, rather aloof and quiet, a minister on leave called Gregoire [Gheorghe] Duca'. Duca held a number of diplo-

King Carol II of Rumania as a young man

matic posts during his career, including Tokyo, Rio de Janeiro, and Washington, DC, and it was he who conducted negotiations with both the American and Soviet embassies in the run up to the coup of August 23, 1944, when King Mi-

Bulci Castle (c. 1934)

chael proclaimed that Rumania was joining the allied forces. Just six months before Leigh Fermor met him, Duca's father (and not his brother, as he writes) Ion Duca was assassinated by Iron Guard fascists, less than a year after the liberally inclined politician had become Rumania's Prime Minister and tried to suppress the ever-growing wave of support for the fascist thugs. It was later even rumoured King Carol himself knew of the assassination plot. Duca

Emperor Charles                    Gheorghe Duca as a young diplomat

had not just alienated the fascists, he was also extremely unpopular when Interior Minister with those who favoured a Habsburg restoration in Rumania and did all in his power to hamper the former Emperor Charles's attempts to drum up support among Habsburg stalwarts eager to place him on the throne of Rumania.

Completing the party from Bulci was Josias von Rantzau and his glamorous girlfriend, Marcelle Catargi. She was from an old Bucharest family and a socialite whose regular appearance in *Tout-Bucharest: Almanach du High Life* suggests

Josias von Rantzau (right)

a character rather different from her more serious diplomat boyfriend, who became a great friend of Leigh Fermor's. Von Rantzau was a descendant of the seventeenth-century Josias von Rantzau, a Danish military leader who became Marshal of France. He was born in 1903 in Schwerin once capital of the Free State of Mecklenburg-Vorpommern and later part of the GDR. His diplomatic career began at the German Foreign Office in 1928 and his postings included Bucharest, Stockholm, Brussels, London and New York. He became an avowed anti-Hitlerite and was close friends with one of the leading figures from the anti-Hitler opposition, Adam von Trott zu Solz. They met in New York in 1927, and both became members of the Kreslau Circle, a group of Hitler opponents around Helmuth James Count von Moltke.

Further along his journey, in Bucharest, Leigh Fermor met again with von Rantzau. He married Countess Johanna zu Wykradt und Isny in 1941 and had one daughter: Marie Gabrielle von Rantzau. She married Prince Friedrich Karl zu Hohenlohe-Waldenburg-Schillingsfürst, bringing another Leigh Fermor noble connection to the fore because the prince's mother, Princess Mechtilde von Urach, was a cousin of Mariga Guinness, related through marriage to Leigh Fermor's hosts in Ireland where he got into trouble at the hunt ball in 1953. In 1944 von Rantzau was back in Bucharest as Counselor at the German Legation. He had been in contact with Raoul Wallenberg in Budapest and both were arrested in September 1944 and sent to Russian prison camps. Von Rantzau was convicted as a spy by the Soviets in 1948 and sent to one of the forced labour camps near the city of Vorkuta, north of the Arctic Circle, a city notoriously associated with the Gulag system since the early 1930s. He died there in 1950.

With the departure of this elegant party from Bucharest—'How smart they are,' said Countess Tinka, 'they make one feel rather rustic and dowdy'—Leigh Fermor's time at the Teleki house was drawing to a close. He whittled away some more happy days with Count Jenő in the library until one morning the Countess came in looking troubled. Her mother was fading fast and the house was about to become a place of mourning. Arrangements had been made to pass Leigh Fermor onward to friends at a neighbouring estate to the east at a place called Zam. This was his first point of entry into Transylvania proper.

IV

# Transylvania

*Here is this country on the very limits of European civilization, yet possessing institutions and rights, for which the most civilized have not been thought sufficiently advanced.*

John Paget, *Hungary and Transylvania*


# Xenia

His journey east from Kápolnás ran in a near straight trajectory through a few ancient hamlets which skirted the southern bank of the Maros River before passing through the border of the old principality at the village of Zam. Here a tributary of the Maros called the Zam River discharges into the mother river near the Csernovits estate, his next hospitable destination. The mansion, a six-bay square block of solid neo-classical design, had a welcoming tri-partite *porte-cochère* which had an open loggia for summer entertainments. When Leigh Fermor arrived the house was deserted except for its acting chatelaine, Xenia Csernovits de Mácsa et Kisoroszi, a ravishing twenty-five-year-old dark-haired beauty, who was alone in the house except for a few of the family retainers. She was married at this time to Gábor Betegh de Csíktusnád, scion of an old Transylvanian noble family. Gábor was working in a bank in Déva. When she met Leigh Fermor the relationship appears to have been going through a turbulent phase and she and Leigh Fermor soon became lovers. 'There was something arresting and unforgettable about her ivory complexion and raven hair and wide sloe-black eyes' is he how he re-

The Csernovits mansion at Zam in the early twentieth century

called her. They had already met and danced together at a party at the Telekis' at Kápolnás. When he met her again he was smitten. 'I couldn't stop dogging her footsteps. [...] As it turned out, she was just as rash and impulsive as I was supposed to be, and prompted, I think, by amused affection on her side and rapt infatuation on mine, a light-hearted affinity had sprung up in a flash.' There was also the allure of her Serbian roots and the great distinction of her family, which he had heard spoken of in some of the houses he had already stayed in.

Her family was a collateral branch of the committal line of Csernovits, which came to prominence in the fifteenth century. Xenia's father, Mihály Csernovits de Mácsa et Kisoroszi, was of Serbian origin, and the youngest son of Arzén Csernovits and his wife Róza, née Anastasijević. Xenia's father was immensely popular in the region because an ancestor, Arsenius, had risen against the Turks with Prince

Eugene of Savoy. He and his followers were expelled from Belgrade by the resurgent Turks and scattered to all quarters of the Empire. Xenia's line settled in Zam, where they had extensive lands which, by the time of Leigh Fermor's arrival, were rather diminished in extent through the Rumanian land reforms of the 1920s. But what they lacked in land they made up for in lineage. Her mother, Gerda von Procopius, through *her* mother, Angélica Dadányi de Gyülvesz, was a direct descendant of the Dukes of Mingrelia, Lord High Stewards of Georgia, Governors of Orbeti and Kaeni and hereditary Dukes since 1184 of the dynasty of Samegrelo, an independent principality until it fell to Imperial Russia in 1803. At this time Leigh Fermor was not just making notes on the Hungarian word for the various ranks within the nobility but also noting the number of pearls on the coronet points of each rank. By now he was a consummate connoisseur of the nobility and must have entered a state of genealogical fugue when he discovered his new girlfriend's lineage.

The Csernovits mansion had a melancholy air about it. It is said locally to be haunted by the spirits of dead serfs who died in the construction of an earlier castle on the site built for the Barons Nopcsa. Leigh Fermor would certainly have heard of one member of the family, Baron Ferenc Nopcsa, who like himself was an intrepid traveller. He was very much in the news in his native Transylvania while Leigh Fermor was travelling through. Unlike Leigh Fermor, Baron Nopcsa was homosexual, an expert palaeontologist and favoured spending his time among Albanian hillsmen. Something of a Lawrence of Arabia-like figure, Nopcsa was once mentioned as a possible candidate for King of the Albanians. He died in a Mayerling-like dramatic suicide in Vienna in 1933, first shooting his Albanian male

The exotic Baron Ferenc Nopcsa in Albanian dress

lover and then himself. Leigh Fermor lists in his Green Diary meeting a Count Kendeffy at Hátszeg, about 40 kilometers south of Deva. Here was the burial place of the Nopcsa family and the site of a Catholic church they built in the nineteenth century.

At Zam, dust-coated family portraits in giltwood frames, lit by dim oil lamps, looked down, perhaps disapprovingly, on the lovers beneath. Leigh Fermor and Xenia found greater comfort in the garden which had been developed by Xenia's father, who planted exotic species of trees brought back from his extensive foreign travels. Giving full vent to his romantic recollections Leigh Fermor recalled these trees as 'looking down on the Maros, which the full moon turned to Mercury'. He even managed to summon up a few serenading nightingales singing in the woods to add verisimilitude to his recollections.

With Annamaria from Budapest, now consigned to the fate of recent romantic memory, he focused his attention on Xenia. Leigh Fermor describes a waterside picnic seduction scene and nocturnal visits on horseback to the Csernovits mansion with the high-flown emotional sentimentalism redolent of youthful passion recalled in middle age. The suspension of disbelief often proves a useful aid to enjoying great travel writing. In reading Leigh Fermor it sometimes becomes a *sine qua non*. Leaving the individual self-aggrandizing youthful seductions scenes aside, few can deny that Patrick Leigh Fermor was one of the great prose stylists of his generation. He has left us one of the most engaging and brilliantly observed portraits of this ancient class on the eve of its extinction. Dervla Murphy, emphasizing this point, has observed of Leigh Fermor's writing, 'it doesn't matter a damn whether he is describing it as he remembers it in 1934 or in 1964 or simply as he fancies it might have been in 1634'.

The seductions all make for colourful copy and there may even be more than a modicum of truth in some of them. However, Xenia's niece by marriage, Stefania Betegh, doubts that the affair with Xenia ever happened. She has no particular reason to defend Xenia's honour. She is not, after all, a direct blood relative. There is also the issue of the confused manner in which Leigh Fermor attempts to disguise, and yet not disguise, Xenia's identity in *Between the Woods and the Water*. At one point in the narrative he gives her full name, the location of her family house at Zam and enough detail for us to know exactly who she is. Then he disguises her as 'Angela' and even adds a footnote about the need to 'alter names' having already made her one of the most identifiable characters in the book and naming her family in the index. She seems not to have been bothered by any of this and when, in her seventy-sixth year, she read the book, she wrote to Leigh Fermor to say how much she had enjoyed it.

Leigh Fermor's attraction for women and his success as a seducer is well known. The balance of probability in the seduction stakes most likely rests with his success with Xenia. The way he writes about her in *Between the Woods and the Water* indicates that he was very much attracted to her at this time. 'Our feelings—mine, anyhow—had run deeper than we admitted, and for as long as it lasted involvement was total. [...] Our short time together had been filled with unclouded delight.' It was one of the last really happy periods of her life as the free spirit in her was now curtailed by marriage. She married Gábor Betegh in 1934 and their daughter Maria Betegh de Csíktusnád was born in 1936. Maria married Count Mihály Teleki, who was the elder son of Count Mihály Teleki of Marosvásárhely (Târgu Mureș). Maria's mother-in-law was Countess Erzsébet Tisza de Borosjenő et Szeged, daughter of Kálmán Tisza, Prime Minister of Hungary and sister of Count István Tisza, who also became Prime Minister of Hungary.

Xenia, despite her reputation for being something of a free spirit, was anxious to keep her friendship with Leigh Fermor secret. After all, he was a mere lad of nineteen and she a recently married woman of twenty-five living within the confines of a formal lifestyle which expected women of her class to conform. Xenia's kinsman, the author Miklós Vajda, recalled her as 'very much a free spirit and a woman with something of the exotic in her looks and nature'. Men found her irresistible. Her affair with Leigh Fermor, has made her more than a mere footnote in twentieth-century travel literature. Just five years after the affair with Leigh Fermor ended she left her husband and family permanently and went to live in Buda with her brother, Arzen Csernovits, a successful horse trainer and breeder. Xenia did not see her daughter again until the turbulent year of 1956. It is understandable that her daughter, Maria, Countess Teleki, who today lives in Munich, is unhappy about the way she was treated by her mother and the memories of that time are still painful for her.

Once Hungary had become a post-war Soviet satellite state, Xenia's life was altered in a way which was unimaginable in 1934. As a 'class enemy' she was deported from a villa at 16 Tulipán utca in Buda, with two Betegh in-laws in 1951. Xenia was sent to Tiszasüly on the Northern Great Plain where she was put to work in rice fields which were being developed, with the aid of slave labour, into Central Europe's biggest rice paddy fields. Her brother Arzén and her eighty-year-old mother were deported with her. Later Xenia was sent back to Budapest and put to work in a textile factory called Textilmintázó, a Soviet-style cooperative which did not survive the fall of Communism and closed soon after in 1992. She spent most of her last years in a squalid little flat which she shared with another woman until eventually, after a blazing row, she accidentally and unintentionally killed her by strangulation on December 20, 1969. This unfortunate event happened after a row with her flatmate over a leasehold interest held by Mrs Ödön Takács from whom she was subletting the former maid's room in an apartment in the then sub-divided tenement building. There had also been an ongoing dispute between the two women over various matters to do with domestic issues in the apartment. She was forced to move from her Buda residence to this apartment by the Communist authorities in 1957. Mrs Takács was in the habit of waking Xenia up in the middle of the night to complain at what she might interpret as the slightest misdemeanour.

A contemporary newspaper account of the incident in *Népszava* from Saturday, January 31, 1970, reveals the tragedy of the incident from both women's perspective. It is also interesting from the viewpoint of the easing of reporting restrictions under 'goulash' Communism in Hungary. Even ten years previously no such crime would have been reported because there was, of course, no criminal activity in a perfect Soviet state: 'Distraught, her hands bleeding, sixty-year-old Mrs Gábor Betegh—an ironer at a co-operative—rang a doorbell at 48 Rajk László utca in the thirteenth district. '"Something terrible has happened," she sobbed. In the hall of Flat 2 on the first floor lay the body of sixty-seven-year-old Mrs Ödön Takács who rented the flat. After a police examination Mrs Betegh was taken to police headquarters and placed under preliminary arrest on suspicion of murder. Investigation into her case has just been finished.'

Mrs Takács rented the two-room flat. Mrs Betegh had lived with her for thirteen years. According to witnesses the long-suffering Xenia—who was often the object of the notoriously disagreeable Mrs Takács's temper—rented the small maid's room adjoining the kitchen from Mrs Takács for 450 forints a month.

In 1968 Mrs Takács gave up her rights as principal lessee in favour of her four-year-old grandchild who lived elsewhere in a two bedroom flat with his parents. Nevertheless she continued to collect rent from Xenia and continued to treat her in the same abusive manner as she had while she was still the principal lessee.

Xenia then reported to the local council that the grandson had never lived in the flat. After hearing the witnesses, the council of the thirteenth district declared the transfer of the rental rights to the grandson to have been illegal, and furthermore stated that Mrs Takács and the two sub-letters were illegal remaining occupants.

From this moment on relations between Mrs Takács and Xenia became truly envenomed. It was within this context that the fateful morning arrived: Mrs Takács once again started abusing Xenia, who twice left the flat to avoid further confrontation. When she returned the second time, Mrs Takács continued the quarrel in the hall and picked up a manicure scissor, 'I will put your eyes out', she screamed at Xenia and made threatening gestures with the scissor in front of the latter's eyes. When Xenia put up her arms in a protective gesture to shield her eyes, Mrs Takács struck several times wounding her hands with the scissor. At the sight of blood Xenia lost control and strangled the woman.

After she was arraigned for manslaughter and served two years imprisonment, Xenia moved to a dark basement flat in the same street. Such was her popularity with her neighbours that many of them testified in court to the justification

The exterior of the apartment building which Xenia was relocated to during the Communist era

The Csernovits house at Zam, today a psychiatric home

of her actions, claiming the victim was an unbearable woman who had disagreed with everyone in the building about every petty matter. This helped lead to leniency in sentencing. Xenia kept in contact with Leigh Fermor intermittently by letter until her death. Her last letter to him is very moving and in it she recalls the days of lost youth and how grey had by then replaced the once raven black of her hair.

This end of Budapest's Pannonia Street, where Xenia's flat was located, is more chipped and faded in appearance than the more prosperous commercial stretch further south, which is guarded by the elegant façade of the Vígszínház— the city's Comedy Theatre. This neighbourhood of the thirteenth district, called Újlipótváros (New Leopoldstown), was still a very new part of the city when Leigh Fermor first came to Budapest in 1934. It soon established itself as home to the literary and artistic set and also formed part of the residential area favoured by some of Budapest's Jewish community. Standing outside 48 Pannonia utca, one can imagine it has changed very little since Xenia Csernovits moved here in 1957. By this time it had been renamed Rajk László utca after an unfortunate but stalwart Communist who fell victim to one of Mátyás Rákosi's Stalinist purges in 1949. It was here in the late 1980s that the once raven-haired siren of Zam, descendant of Dukes and nobles of ancient Georgia, ended her days far from the stately grandeur of the family mansion at Zam.

# 'István'

The closest male bond Leigh Fermor formed in Transylvania, and indeed on the entire walk, was with Elemér von Klobusiczky. 'István', in *Between the Woods and the Water*, had been in a Hussar regiment during the Great War. He was tall, striking rather than good looking, had a military bearing, and was an expert horseman and an excellent shot. He was sixteen years older than Leigh Fermor and there was something of the older brother, and not a little hero worship in their relationship. There was also something of the ex-soldiers world of derring-do, bravado and gasconade about him, which appealed hugely to the young Leigh Fermor. It is not difficult to see how a dashing ex-Hussar, who still kept his uniform in mothballs, might appeal to a romantic nineteen-year-old. Fifty years later he could still recall this snippet of military description from Elemér's stock of such tales: 'You should have seen us moving off for Galicia and Bukovina,' he said. 'The uhlans in their square czapkas and red trousers, dragoons in long Waffenrocks, and the hussars like us in pale blue.'

The Klobusiczky family estate at Guraszáda lay to the east of the lands of their friends and neighbours the Csernovits of Zam. The nearest large settlement to the village is Dobra and beyond that further to the east is the historic town of Déva. The Klobusiczky family married into the lands at Guraszáda in the late nineteenth century when a daughter of the former landlords of the area, the Benedicty de Benedekfalva family, married Elemér's father, Andor Klobusiczky de Klobusicz et Zétény. He was still living at Guraszáda with his wife, Alexandrine, when Leigh Fermor came to stay. At one time the family had extensive estates in Felső-Magyarország, or Upper Hungary, as Slovakia was then known, and they had been prominent in the region since the fourteenth century. Peter Klobusiczky (1754–1843), Archbishop of Kalocsa, gave away a vast portion of the family fortune to help the needy. Their town palace still stands in the centre of Eperjes (Prešov), the ancient family crest, with its skyward-pointing arrow, as Leigh Fermor noted, still adorning the building today. The family was ennobled by the Anjou kings and were given land in Klobusic (Klobušice)—hence the surname.

There was much talk of military matters between Elemér and Leigh Fermor. He even convinced his host to put on his old uniform so that he might draw his portrait dressed in this finery. Perhaps it didn't even take too much convincing. When Leigh Fermor told him about a desire he once had to join the Indian Army, Elemér looked at him misty-eyed and said, 'I'd have loved that! Could I do it now, do you think?' Elemér's thoughts, spurred on by his young friend's genuine interest, may have allowed him late-night indulgence in visions of himself at the head of a fearless body of Bengal Lancers. However, the reality was his sense of duty kept him firmly rooted in his family estate in Guraszáda. It was the Carpathians, and not the Himalayas, which in the cold light of day formed the frontier of his bailiwick.

Elemér sketched in uniform by PLF

His military days were never far from Elemér's thoughts
and their nights were spent chatting about the glory days
of Transylvanian history and particularly the role played by
the Irish in Austro-Hungarian Empire. 'An Irish O'Donnell
had been Governor of Transylvania in the 18th century,' he
tells us in *Between the Woods and the Water*. Can his friend
Elemér have told him this? Conal, in the Irish version of
his name, Karl in the Austrian, O'Donnell was Inspector-
General of Cavalry in the Imperial Austrian Army, and indeed was Governor of Transylvania, and recipient of the
Grand Cross of the Military Order of Maria Theresa for
gallantry at the Battle of Torgau in 1761. An O'Donnell
too had been headmaster of Elemér's old school in Vienna, the Theresianum—the Eton of Austria, as some have

The Klobusiczky crest above the entrance door of the eighteenth-century family palace in Prešov. PLF writes of 'the skyward-pointing arrow'

called it. Elemér's schooldays were recalled later in Leigh Fermor's journey when he stayed with a former classmate of his, Heinz Schramm, near Herkulesfürdő (Băile Herculane), the Baths of Hercules. He recalled him as 'a marvelous fellow but a bit too proud of his five-pointed coronet'. Another O'Donnell was also recalled. Count Maximilian O'Donnell, was hailed as a hero of the Empire for saving the life of the young, Emperor Francis Joseph when a Hungarian journeyman tailor called János Libényi tried to assassinate him in Vienna in 1853. Leigh Fermor was still playing the Irish card very much to his advantage.

The house at Guraszáda was architecturally undistinguished. It was a classic plain manor house of a once prosperous Transylvanian noble family. The special charm of the rectangular, one-storey structure lay in the fact that three sides of the house had a wrap-around columned arcade from which the park and arboretum could be admired in all seasons. Inside there was a 40-square-metre drawing room. The gate columns and decorative urns of which Leigh Fermor writes have disappeared in recent years but the house still stands. It served as an agricultural institute during Communism. Today in stands close to collapse but not totally beyond saving if something is done within the next year or so. The door with the coloured glass fanlight still gives access to the rear terrace but the river view of which he writes is now totally occluded by overgrown trees.

The estate was, in 1934, already greatly reduced in size due to the post-war Rumanian land reforms, as was the case of the land holdings of many of his hosts in this part of the world. Leigh Fermor observes that despite an abundance of servants there appeared to be very little ready cash. But of

Guraszáda today

all the houses he visited on his walk, it was the one where he was made to feel most at home. Here he was truly made welcome like an adopted family member. Elemér and he got on so well that his host tried to convince him to stay for a year, with enticements such as fox hunting with Count Wesselényi's pack. 'But I have no money,' Leigh Fermor said. 'Neither have I,' replied his host.

Elemér's house as PLF would have known it

Elemér's house as it stands today

Leigh Fermor heard some talk of recent political history at Guraszáda. He was intrigued by the fact Elemér may once have been on the hit list of Tibor Szamuely, who was made People's Commissar for Military Affairs in the short-lived Hungarian Soviet Republic of 1919 under the leadership of Béla Kun. Szamuely was responsible for the so-called 'Red Terror' which he ruthlessly directed against anyone whom he saw as an 'enemy of the people'. Such was his devotion to expiation by blood letting that he delivered with gusto the following remarks at Győr on April 20, 1919:

> Power has fallen into our hands. Those who wish the old regime to return, must be hung without mercy. We must bite the throat of such individuals. The victory of the Hungarian Proletariat has not cost us major sacrifices so far. But now the situation demands that blood must flow. We must not be afraid of blood. Blood is steel: it strengthens our hearts, it strengthens the fist of the Proletariat. Blood will make us powerful. Blood will lead us to the true world of the Commune. We will exterminate the entire bourgeoisie if we have to!

It has also been suggested by Leigh Fermor that Elemér may have been involved in the 'White Terror' which succeeded the rise to power of Admiral Horthy, though it was soon suppressed by him as a threat to the political stability of his Regency. If there is any truth in Elemér's involvement it was most likely to have been both peripheral and minimal because he was able to live openly in Hungary when the Communist regime came to power after World War II. Many of the army officers who were heavily involved in the 'White Terror', fearing recrimination by the new regime, left Hungary in 1945. At a time when the Hungarian State

Protection Department, known as the ÁVO was being run by the notoriously brutal Gábor Péter, Elemér did not appear to suffer any more than other members of his class, so the claim to his involvement in the 'White Terror' may have only a grain of truth in it.

One of the few contemporary political events which impinged on his visit also happened before leaving Guraszáda. It was in Transylvania that Leigh Fermor claimed to have heard of the assassination of Dollfuss. Barely a year earlier, the 'Little Chancellor' had paid his respects to the remains of Count Albert Apponyi, as his funeral train from Geneva passed through Vienna on its way to Budapest. The shooting of the Austrian Chancellor by a group of Nazi sympathisers on July 25, 1934, presaged the annexation of Austria by Hitler four years later. The young Leigh Fermor quite understandably had other preoccupations at the time.

Apart from their shared military interests and fantasies, Elemér and Leigh Fermor had one other interest which united them in friendship. That was their boundless interest in the pursuit of beautiful girls. Leigh Fermor describes a waterside picnic, a seduction scene and nocturnal visits to the Csernovits mansion at Zam with the high-flown sentimentalism redolent of youthful passion recalled in middle age. This might also apply to the other riverside seduction scene of two peasant girls which is described in great detail in *Between the Woods and the Water.* He writes of how he and Elemér are seduced from a river swim by the taunts of these gorgeous rustic hay-making nymphs, he calls Safta and Illena, and how they end up tumbling in the hay-stacks in a manner reminiscent of eighteenth-century lords of the manor exercising the *droit de seigneur.* They were forced to hurry back to the house to be just in time to have dinner with no less grand fellow guests than a Bishop and a Countess. 'The thin and jeweled fingers of the iron-grey shingled Gräfin were crossed in her lap and the purple sash of the Bishop glowed in the lamp light. [...] The Gräfin unfolded her napkin and shook it loose with a twinkle of sapphires.'

During his stay with Elemér, Countess Tinka Teleki's mother died. Leigh Fermor travelled by train with Elemér and Xenia to the funeral service at Kápolnás. A horse and carriage was waiting at the train station at Soborsin, where they alighted for the short onward journey to the house. When they arrived they went immediately to the entrance hall where the coffin lay open. It was the first time Leigh Fermor had seen a dead body. The service was conducted by three Uniate priests and the air in the entrance hall where the service was held hung heavy with the smell of sacred incense. After the entombment of the old countess in the family vault, lunch was provided and Leigh Fermor was greeted like an old family friend, making him remark, 'I felt I had known them all for ever.'

Back at Guraszáda he felt it was time for him to pack his rucksack. By the time he left, the Feast Day of Saint Stephen was approaching. St István's day, August 20, officially marks the end of high summer in Hungary. The time had come for him to leave behind his closest Hungarian friend and move along the road towards his final destination. He did so with an air of both regret and expectation.

Before taking his final leave of Xenia and Elemér, he presents the reader with one of his greatest and most controversial *madeleine*s in which the narrative is imperfectly matched to the actual facts. In a chapter called 'Triple Fugue' he describes the three friends setting out on a road trip together across the interior of Transylvania. The veracity or otherwise of the journey has confused Leigh Fermor enthusiasts for many years. However, the late Rudi Fischer claimed Leigh Fermor told him he made up much of the detail of the motor journey from a book about Transylvania lent him by his Budapest mentor. This can be confirmed by a letter to Fisher which Leigh Fermor wrote him on November 22, 1984, in which he confides his 'guilty secret, which you are the only living soul to share'. This is his admission of the fact that the whole journey was a fabrication based also on a later visit to Transylvania in the 1980s. 'Triple Fugue' is Leigh Fermor's writing at its best and was one of his own favourite parts of the book. He felt so utterly obliged to maintain the reader's interest by simply not just 'plodding along' that when he confessed to Fisher what he had done, he asked him to burn the letter. Fortunately he did not and we are left with this brilliant account of one travel writer's' craft and methodology and a feeling of sympathy for his plight as he struggles with his conscience. 'My moral decline is such', he wrote Fischer, 'that in this particular case, I am rather shocked to discover that I don't really give a damn about my misconduct; it has enabled me to include so much I would have had to jettison, while doing nobody any harm at all, [...] I would hate this evidence of wickedness to be extant. Dr Johnson says that nobody writing lapidary inscriptions is on oath. I would like to extend it to a *certain category* of events, *under very special circumstances if they are half-a-century old*'.

The recent discovery of a photograph of the car, which he claimed they 'borrowed' from László Lázár, a friend of Elemér's, who lived less than fifteen miles from Guraszáda, shows the vehicle exactly as described by Leigh Fermor and demonstrates the lengths he went to in order to add veracity to the story. He saw it when he stayed at the Lázár house in 1934 and remembered it exactly. 'The borrowed vehicle was an old-fashioned, well-polished touring car with

room for all three in front. It had a canvas hood with a cel-
luloid window in the back.' There are also some addresses listed in the 1934 'Green Diary' for people who lived in
the city he names as 'Klausenburg'. To the Saxons it was
Klausenburg; known 'inexpugnable and immutably' to the
Hungarians as Kolozsvár, and to the Rumanians it will be
forever Cluj. Registering people's names in his diary was
usually solid enough evidence of having been to a place on
his journey but not in this instance. The Klausenburg addresses he added in 1934 were a Baron Kemény and a Countess Paula Bethlen, whom he had met elsewhere. He even
carried the fiction to such a convincing degree that he pretended to have written to Elemér in the 1980s when working on *Between the Woods and the Water* to ask where they
had returned the car to its owner. The city was supposed
to be their end stop on what was presented as a clandestine
trip—so that Xenia's honour might not be compromised
by meeting neighbours. Tamás Barcsay, whose family estate is at Gyalu, some twenty kilometres west of Kolozsvár, has been able to identify the house, indeed the very
bedroom which Leigh Fermor and Xenia were supposed
to have shared in the city. The house belonged at one time
to the family of Barcsay's friend, Countess Hanna Mikes,
who had befriended Tom and Unity Mitford in Hungary.
It is located not far from the house where one of Hungary's
most beloved kings, Matthias Corvinus, was born in 1443.
The house is on what is today called Piaţa Muzeului and in
1934 was known as Piaţa Carolina. It was in the Breakfast
Room of the Mikes house where Leigh Fermor invented a
servant informing them of the assassination of the Austrian
Chancellor Dollfuss but 'the gloom didn't last much longer
than breakfast'. It was also from a bedroom of this house
that he invents the notion of Xenia and his young self be-

ing awakened by the elegantly imagined discord of 'the reciprocally schismatic bells' of the city; this wonderful description indicating Leigh Fermor's perfect understanding
of the very ethnically mixed composition of the religions of
Kolozsvár's inhabitants in those pre-Ceauşescu days. However, it was in 1982 during Ceauşescu's reign that he first
visited the city.

He mentions the Bánffy Palace in Kolozsvár's main
square, today a museum of fine art. In 1934 it was still a
private residence where Xenia or Elemér would have been
known to the servants and a discreet tip would most likely have secured entry, even if the family was not in residence. Leigh Fermor carried the ruse off so successfully he
pretended to be very excited about being in a house where
Liszt had given recitals. At the outbreak of the Great War,
an English governess, Florence Tarring, was stranded in the
Bánffy Palace from where she wrote long discursive letters
to her sister in England describing the situation during the
war and after the Rumanian occupation of Transylvania.

Their fictional visit to the Hotel New York—where the

The car 'borrowed' by PLF, Xenia and Elemér for the trip to Kolozsvár (Cluj)

Hotel New York, Kolozsvár (Cluj)

'barman had invented an amazing cocktail—only surpassed by the one called "Flying" in the Vier Jahreszeiten bar in Munich'—was created after his stay in the hotel in 1982. His brilliant description of drinking cocktails, which 'we sipped with misgiving and delight among a Regency neo-Roman décor of cream and ox-blood and gilding: Corinthian capitals spread their acanthus leaves and trophies of quivers, and hunting horns, lyres and violins were caught up with festoons between the pilasters' fits perfectly the abandoned interior as it stands today awaiting a new beginning.

The Hotel New York has had a sorry history since its glamorous days, becoming the Nazi HQ in the city during World War II. Throughout Communism it was named 'The Continental' and today it is closed down, awaiting its re-birth hopefully along with the reincarnation of the 'demon-barman', that expert shaker of lethal cocktails, when it will once again bear its old name.

Leigh Fermor's description of Kolozsvár in 1934 is largely taken from a book lent him by Rudi Fischer. Walter Starkie, the brilliant Anglo-Irish scholar, tutor to Samuel Beckett at

The Hotel New York where PLF and Xenia enjoyed a fictional tryst and cocktail. Today awaiting restoration.

Trinity College, Dublin, and godson of Oscar Wilde's Trinity tutor Sir John Pentland Mahaffy, had walked through Hungary and Rumania in 1929–30. Like Leigh Fermor he too kept a diary and in 1933 published one of the best travel books on the region called *Raggle-Taggle: Adventures with a Fiddle in Hungary and Roumania*. Starkie, like Leigh Fermor, shared a common liking for the conflicting partisans who make up the old Hungarian and Rumanian divide. Much of Leigh Fermor's fictional car journey is taken from Starkie's book but is imbued with so much of his feeling for the region, that, coupled with the fact he did visit the area in the early 1980s, we can again invoke Dervla Murphy's defence of the writer to suspend disbelief without feeling, one hopes, too beguiled by the subterfuge.

The moment of actual departure from Xenia finally came. He claims they parted at Déva railway station where Xenia boarded a train which would take her to Keleti Station, Budapest's eastern terminus. We cannot be certain of the exact point of departure but he does give a very charming account of how he recollects it. 'Our farewells had been made and I can still feel the dust on her smooth cheek' is how he recalls what was to be his last ever sighting of her as she leaned out of the carriage window. The journey would take her back via many of the places Leigh Fermor had passed through since he left Budapest on April 12. He stood watching as she trailed a silk scarf out of the carriage window until the train became only 'a feather of smoke' among the trees of the Maros valley.

He took his leave of Elemér in what would be the penultimate castle stay of the many he had enjoyed since leaving Budapest. Elemér and he made their way some thirty kilometres from Déva to Lapusnak (Lăpuşnic) to their host László Lázár. They spent a few days with this charming and delightfully eccentric nobleman who had been a cowboy in America and a gaucho in the Argentine and even a horseman in a circus when times were tough. The family belonged to the untitled Transylvanian nobility—Leigh Fermor mistakenly assumed László Lázár was a Count. The confusion is easily achieved in a land where being of ancient noble standing still means much more than having what many old Hungarian families still describe as a 'mere Habsburg title'.

His stay at Lapusnak was essentially a bachelor gathering. A neighbour, Count István Horváth Toldi, came over from his estate, Mintia, to make up the party of four men for dinner. He had just come into his inheritance three years previously while his sister inherited a world-famous stamp collection from their father, Rudolf. Leigh Fermor was amused by this all-male society and enjoyed *al fresco* dining served by a pretty Swabian housekeeper 'like a soubrette in an opera'. After dinner Elemér exercised his skill as cocktail party piano player and as usual they sat up late into the night. Like most of Leigh Fermor's hosts in Transylvania, László Lázár suffered terribly at the hands of the Communists after the war. He was sent to a work camp for three years, his estate was confiscated and his family humiliated as 'class enemies'.

After two days at Lapusnak, Leigh Fermor was ready to take his leave of Elemér and this he did with a heavy heart. At their parting each 'trailed a faint cloud of hangover in opposite directions'. For the first time in many months he was alone again with only the massive bulk of the Carpathians to keep him company until he reached his next destination at Tomeşti—one of the few locations he names in Rumanian. There are three such place names in Rumania. Leigh Fermor's destination is known to Hungarians as Tomesd and is situated in Hunedoara County in western Rumania. It was here he stayed with Robert von Winckler, the man he transformed into that composite character the Polymath of the Wachau. He is presented in the book as a man of a very fine scholarly disposition. He had a superb library in this isolated place and again, as was his habit throughout this journey, Leigh Fermor made good use of it. Hunting trophies decorated the interior of his bachelor quarters and a collection of guns were kept close at hand on a gun rack. Von Winckler was the owner of a rather economically inefficacious glass works, which was in financial difficulties at the time of Leigh Fermor's visit. This is not surprising given his main interests seemed to be scholarship and hunting and over his three day visit he told his young guest many entertaining stores from old Transylvanian lore about wolves and ancient forests. It was here, as he prepared to leave it, that the Stokeresque side of Transylvania makes a conspicuous appearance in his writing. 'All the castles were haunted, and earthly packs of wolves were reinforced after dark by solitary werewolves; vampires were on the move; witches stirred and soared; the legends and fairy stories of a dozen nations piled up. [...] and some of it must have found its way into the bloodstream.' Something else had found its way into his bloodstream and which, he readily admitted, was a taste for the comfort offered by castle hopping. '[N]o more castles the other side of the Danube. These refugees had scattered my path intermittently ever since the Austrian border. Their inhabitants seemed doubly precious now, and I brooded with homesickness on feasts and libraries and stables and endless talk by lamp and candle light.'

There would be just one last comfortable billet on the north side of the Danube before he continued onward towards Constantinople. Elemér had arranged for him to stay with his old school friend, Heinz Schramm, at the Baths of Hercules. By 1934 this ancient spa town was surviving on the memory of its halcyon days as a former major leisure resort on the edge of the Habsburg Empire. It would soon become a pleasure zone for Communist apparatchiks and the elaborate architecture of the Habsburg era would be surrounded by concrete edifices of hideous design. In 1930 a new hotel, the Cerna (called after the local river), was built and it was from here Leigh Fermor telephoned his host. Heinz Schramm was a stout man of jolly disposition and the owner of a large timber works in the district. He lived with his father, a retired admiral from the Austro-

Hungarian Navy. As ever with retired officers, Leigh Fermor was in his element and spent hours with the old sailor, encouraging his reminiscences. He listened enthusiastically to the old man's stories of his secondment to the Royal Navy where he knew Lord Charles Beresford, who had dangled Berta von Berg on his knee when her father had been Governor of Fiume. He talked of balls in Fiume, Pola and Trieste and there was talk too of his old friend Admiral Horthy, whom he remembered as 'a decent sort of chap with not very much going on in the top story'. It was at this time in Pola that James Joyce was supposed to have been Horthy's English-language tutor, perhaps just as apocryphal a tale as Vladimir Ilyich Lenin being taught English by another Irishman. Those last days of high summer were punctuated with picnics and even a ball at the Casino in the town, where Leigh Fermor danced and listened to arias from *The Barber of Seville* sung by a visiting Budapest opera company.

But we must leave him now, before he faces into the final leg of his journey to Constantinople. In Heinz Schramm's drawing room, in a house near the Baths of Hercules, he sits discussing the finer points of what it meant to be 'of noble blood' in the lands between the woods and the water. 'But nobility meant more than heraldic baubles and forms of address,' he observed. 'It signified membership of a legally separate order with a whole array of privileges. These inequities had long ago been removed but a chasm yawned still and much of the ancient aloofness and awe hovered about the descendants of country dynasts.' I once asked Rudi Fischer if he thought Leigh Fermor was an incontrovertible snob. He paused for thought and with an impish smile replied: 'Paddy was blessed with the common touch but he loved a Duke, adored an Archduke and positively worshiped a Grand Duke!' In his youth his exposure to all those

The Transtlvanian Nobility in Exile photo taken at the Piarist Ball
in the Plaza Hotel, New York, December 1960.
Standing L to R: József Barcsay de Nagybarcsa, Countess Erzsébet Révay de
Sklabnica Blatnica et Réva née (Szokoly de Bernece), Éva Barcsay de Nagybarcsa and
her mother Éva Barcsay de Nagybarcsa (née Dezső), Tamás Barcsay de Nagybarcsa.
Seated: L to R: Anna Sándor de Kénos (the last woman living to have met PLF in
Transylvania in 1934) and Mary Szokoly de Bernece.

Hungarian grandees may have turned his head slightly but
in the end his talent for acute observation of his fellow man
coupled with a genuine interest in the history rather than in
the social status of this class, has left us with one of the most
finely wrought portraits in the English language of a society
which was on the point of being annihilated. We must be
forever grateful that an extraordinary young man crossed
the bridge at Esztergom on that Easter Saturday in 1934.

V

Epilogue
# Return
# to
# Budapest

*I have carried the soldier's musket, the traveller's stick,*
*the pilgrim's staff.*

Chateaubriand

It is to the fate of that composite character, Leigh Fermor's greatest Hungarian friend, Elemér/'István' that we now return because he was one of the principal reasons which brought him back to Budapest long after his first visit. In 1943 Elemér married Countess Julia Apponyi de Nagy-Apponyi, a member of one of Hungary's leading political and aristocratic families. Her first husband was Count Ferenc Pálffy ab Erdőd. Her father, Count Albert Apponyi de Nagy-Apponyi, was the revered statesman who did all in his power to resist the breakup of Hungary at the Versailles conference in 1920. On her mother's side she was related to the British royal family. In wartime Budapest she ran a famous *haute couture* house. It was popular with those women who had any money left to spend on personal finery and there were many who had but they were mostly the wives of diplomats. She even designed clothes for Unity Mitford during her 1939 visit to Budapest. During World War II she was a legendary hostess in her house in the *Vár* where she was able to mix the many elements of Budapest social life with considerable social ease. A painting of her by society portraitist Count Gyula Batthyány captures something of the elegance of pre-war Budapest society.

Many of the old Hungarian noble families were quick to adjust to their new post-war status which was essentially that of being impecunious. The twenty-three-year-old Countess Mimi Széchenyi worked as a barmaid in the Hotel Astoria. Mimi's twenty-year-old sister, Countess Alexandra, first worked as an interpreter for the Russians, later as a secretary in the same hotel. *Der Spiegel*, in 1947 remarked that the trade directory for Budapest then looked more like the *Almanach de Gotha*. Many members of the Hungarian nobility spoke several languages. Some were brought up by English or French nannies. Many had German, French and English running fluently alongside their Magyar mother tongue. This Hungarian aristocratic penchant for languages is perfectly caught in Isabel Colgate's *The Shooting Party* when the Hungarian Count Tibor Rakassyi [sic] invites the beautiful daughter of the house to stay at his family estate in Hungary. Her younger brother chips in that his sister can't possibly go because she doesn't speak Hungarian. The Count replies 'neither do we, at home we speak French.' Elemér had fluent French, German and English and turned his hand to translation work. He had one son, Miklós Klobusiczky, with Julia Apponyi in 1946. Miklós married Princess Caroline Murat, a descendant of Napoleon's brother-in-law, the King of Naples. Elemér and Julia divorced soon after the war. Julia Apponyi reopened her *couture* business in 1945 and it enjoyed considerable success until nationalized by the Communists in 1948. She was arrested on Christmas night of that year and sent to a labour camp. She was later deported into the horrendous system of internal exile reserved for 'class enemies'. The scale of these internal exile orders and the vehemence of their execution is reflected in an announcement in the Party mouthpiece *Szabad Nép* (A Free People) in its edition of 15 June 1951 when it trumpeted: "The following undesirable elements were deported from Budapest from 21 May - six former princes, 52 former

Portrait of Countess Julia Apponyi by Count Gyula Batthyány (1930s)

counts, 41 former barons and all of their families". Together with these aristocrats nearly 500 of former administrators in the Horthy regency and dozens of army officers, 30 factory owners, 46 bankers, 93 wholesale merchants 105 landowners were also deported. All aristocrats had the only title they would be recognised by henceforth place before their name and that was 'former'. The newspaper also announced that their property would be seized for the benefit of 'mainly industrial workers with big families'. It failed to mention that the biggest apartments in the best parts of Budapest would be reserved for the Party elite.

Elemér found work as a technical advisor in stone quarries outside Vác, some thirty-five kilometres north of Budapest. He made a dash for the border in 1956 but failed to cross into Austria and like so many other attempted escapees or 'fencers' as they were known, he was apprehended and imprisoned. After his release, he made a meagre living as a translator but essentially he was trapped behind the Iron Curtain. Known to friends as 'Globus', he was never taken seriously by those who knew him very well. There was something of the joker and fantasist in his nature, which Leigh Fermor captures in the book. For example, his daydreaming about joining the Indian Army. When his fortunes began to wane in the late 1930s he began to move about, staying with friends in various places. Sándor Betegh remembers Elemér stayed at his grandparents' estate at Zsibót in southern Hungary near Szigetvár, the last resting place of the heart of Suleiman the Magnificent. Once Communism had taken a grip on Hungary, Elemér found a new role as the go-between for the sale of the remaining few trinkets which belonged to his fellow aristocrats. Unlike many of his class he had the common touch and was able to wheel and deal with the purchasers of gold, silver and china, often securing better deals for his friends and protecting them from the black market sharks who were circling around their few remaining possessions. Anna Sándor, who had been a neighbour of Elemér's in Transylvania remembers him as being 'rather pompous and something of a wheeler-dealer'.

Leigh Fermor returned to Budapest in 1965 on a commission from *Holiday* magazine which involved visiting many of the places he had seen in 1934 but now it was to be in the guise of a Danube journey. He saw some old friends and was pleased to see Budapest a happier place than many of its surrounding neighbours. His portrait was painted at this time by János Szegfű. It appears the artist wished to finish the painting but Leigh Fermor was unable to wait. However, the resulting image is a good likeness of the middle-aged man. He returned to Budapest again in the period of Hungary's history now known as *gulyáskommunizmus* or goulash Communism. He visited Budapest in 1978 and met Elemér again for the first time since they parted in August 1934. Elemér was then living in Buda at 127 Pasareti út in the once fashionable and prosperous suburb near the Rózsadomb by then populated by senior Communist functionaries, as it still is today by their descendants. He was then working as a translator of scientific documents for the government. With Elemér and his sister Ilona, whom he had also known in Transylvania in 1934, he motored to Esztergom and Visegrád. He also visited the old von Berg house at 15 Úri utca, then still occupied by tenants placed there after the house was sequestered by the Communist authorities in 1951 when the von Bergs were evicted. Apparently he received the 'cold shoulder' welcome typical of the times and was unable to get a foot past the front door.

He arrived in the city again on May 6, 1982, when Hungary was then known for some years as 'the happiest barracks in the East Bloc camp'. This refers to the late Kadarist period when the country was viewed, especially by some of its more unfortunate Communist neighbours, as being less under the Soviet kosh, or megalomaniacal Communist leadership style, than they were. The city was so packed with visitors because of some conference that there were no hotel rooms available and he stayed in a private flat. This seemed to suit him very well because the owner turned out to be 'a frightfully pretty fair-haired girl called Aggy', as he informed Debo Devonshire in a letter.

Leigh Fermor has sometimes been criticized for abandoning his Hungarian friends, especially midst the harsh crackdown in the period immediately following the 1956 Revolution. This is both inaccurate and unfair. He did his best through British diplomatic contacts in Budapest and later through Rudi Fischer to ascertain how his Hungarian friends were doing in this period. He was also aware that any direct traceable contact with them was likely to have serious consequences, given that by then he had a high public profile as a former officer in British Military Intelligence whose wartime activities had even been turned into a Hollywood movie, *Ill Met by Moonlight* starring Dirk Bogarde as Leigh Fermor. It was based on a factual account of SOE (Special Operations Executive) activities in Crete. The book by Leigh Fermor's friend and fellow officer W. Stanley Moss attracted much praise at the time of publication in 1950. However the movie was looked on somewhat disdainfully by some former SOE officers who saw the whole exercise as being rather 'flash' and not quite the done thing.

He also managed to maintain contact with some of his former Hungarian connections through new friends who had married into some of the Hungarian families he met in 1934. One such was Charlotte Szapáry (née Star Busmann). The daughter of a Dutch diplomat she married László Szapáry the son of Count Frigyes Szapáry and Princess Maria Hedwig zu Windisch-Graetz. He endeared himself to Charlotte by swallowing one of her pearl earrings during a date at Fortnum & Mason in the mid 1950s. She was also friends with Lucien Freud who apparently swallowed the other of the pair of earrings. Despite such, or perhaps because of such antics, she and Leigh Fermor were still corresponding until shortly before his death in 2011. Charlotte Szapáry lived in the Waldviertel in northwestern Austria from where she kept in touch with some of her friends still living in Budapest in the dying days of Communism.

Even in the early 1980s in Budapest, the old fears from Stalinist times still lingered, especially in the generation then in their seventies as many of Charlotte Szapáry's friends would then have been. It was not to be unexpected that they might still be concerned about the possibility of the old Communist scare tactic, the midnight ring on the doorbell—*csengő frász* in Hungarian. Bearing this in mind, he met Elemér discreetly in Budapest on that 1982 visit. Elemér was then eighty-three and living in a soulless Soviet-style tenement block in Centenarium, east of Pest. He called there and took him out to lunch. Elemér had had a hard life under the Communist regime, especially in the Stalinist period. Even after Stalin's death he was still feeling the wrath of the authorities. In 1954 he was arraigned before the district court in Budapest on a trumped-up charge of fraud and forgery against a factory in the city of Pécs. These alleged criminal charges were a regular feature of life for the so-called Hungarian 'class enemies' under the tough regime of Mátyás Rákosi, a zealous Stalinist, once described by the *Daily News* correspondent in Vienna, John Gunther, as 'the most malevolent character I have ever met in political life'. Gunther had seen most of the tyrants of the 1930s at very close range, working alongside such legendary correspondents as G.E.R. Gedye of the *Daily Telegraph*. The charge against Elemér was proven in court and he spent the next two years in prison but was released during the 1956 revolution. His friend Count Gyula Batthyány faced similar trumped-up charges after the war. He was taken from his family estate and sent to live in his former servants' house. He was not as fortunate as Elemér and was sentenced to eight years in prison and deprived of all of his assets. He died in 1959 in a mental hospital in Budapest.

After his visit to Budapest Leigh Fermor went off on a tour of some of the old houses in the Puszta, the Banat and Transylvania in which he had stayed in 1934. They included Elemér's old house at Guraszáda, by then a government experimental plant nursery. Rarely one to miss the opportunity to embroider the facts a little, he described the house in a letter to Debo Devonshire as 'a big, late medieval place'—which it actually was not. It was a typical Hungarian manor house of the middle size—the sort of grand large bungalow which Lutyens designed for prosperous members of the Raj in India.

Sadly today the house is showing signs of neglect, though it could be saved if there was a will to do so. It was not claimed back under Rumania's generous restitution laws and now belongs to the local village administration. One can still just about make out the shape of the formal gardens and in the window frames are some surviving panes of the stained glass described in *Between the Woods and the Water*. Elemér's coat of arms is no longer in place over the entrance archway. During his last visit Leigh Fermor met some locals who remembered Elemér and they offered him some plum *pálinka*, a prized traditional Hungarian *eau de vie*, made out of the former landlord's plums, an act for which they apologized. They also apologized for living on his property and sent him their kind regards. No one suggested giving up any of the objects they had looted from the house when the estate had been sequestered by the Communists.

On that same road trip in 1982, Leigh Fermor also drove over a thousand kilometres around the Great Hungarian Plain, visiting some of the houses where he had been a guest long ago. 'A series of minor Bridesheads' as he somewhat over-enthusiastically described the houses to Debo Devonshire. He found no trace of any of the former inhabitants of these *schlosses* except for a chance meeting with Count Hansi von Meran who had been a boy of twelve when he had visited their house at Körösladány. Count Hansi was arrested after the war and held in Soviet captivity for ten years in a Siberian Gulag. It had not broken his spirit and Leigh Fermor described him thus: 'He was enormously tall when I saw him now, Marie Antoinette's biggest gt. gt. gt. gt. nephew, grizzled and rather weather-beaten, rather shy with very nice blue eyes.' Marci von Meran was visiting her brother when Leigh Fermor called. He last saw her forty-eight years previously. She was now a great-grandmother. She reminded him of his mornings spent in the old house, writing in 'a big green book' at a Biedermeier table which they had managed to rescue from the looters of their old family home, along with a portrait of their kinswoman, the Empress Maria Theresa. It was all rather sad but it reaffirmed for Leigh Fermor the value of his writing, as a first-hand witness, to an entirely lost way of life. He also visited Ókigyós and Zam on this trip and commented on the sheer weight of the melancholia of seeing the place where he had his affair with Xenia. It was then occupied by unfortunate psychiatric patients, still victims of the last years of Ceauşescu's hideous regime. It is still thus occupied today.

It is interesting to note that no file exists on Leigh Fermor in the archives of the Hungarian Secret Service. We will never be sure if one did exist, however, because a great deal of material was lost in the immediate post-communist period when many files were destroyed. If one did not exist he must have been extremely careful in covering his movements for this to be the case. Perhaps it was his old SOE training coming in useful. It does seem extraordinary that there is no file on him, given that the Hungarian Secret Service was particularly interested in English visitors to Budapest. They had a network of Hungarian informers in London who often suggested names of people they might watch or indeed try to recruit. Churchill's biographer, the historian Martin Gilbert, was approached by the Hungarian Secret Service in the 1960s with a view to recruiting him as a Communist spy. There are extensive files on him in Budapest. There are also files on Elemér and Xenia and they feature in the files of others. We learn from the file of Countess Margit Teleki that Elemér proposed marriage to her after her husband Count László Bethlen left Hungary but that she thought him too much of a drunk to accept his proposal. Sadly, Margit Teleki, succumbed to pressure to spy on her fellow aristocrats and became a very valuable source for the Hungarian Communist Intelligence Service in their efforts to keep an eye on the old noble families. She had attempted to flee Hungary in 1956 but her escape plan was betrayed by her own daughter, Jolán, who then also became an operative for the State Security Service. The information these two aristocratic women provided about their fellow aristocrats, by now, of course, "enemies of the people" makes for sad reading, especially when one considers that Jolán was the great-niece of one of Hungary's most distinguished Prime Ministers, Count István Bethlen, who served from 1921 to 1931 and that her mother was the sister of Gemma Teleki who was forced to live in a broom cupboard by the Communists. Margit was also a kinswoman of another Prime Minister, Pál Teleki, who entertained Leigh Fermor several times in Budapest.

Leigh Fermor did not return to Budapest again until October 1985. This time he came armed with a typescript of *Between the Woods and the Water*. He was anxious to show this

The author with PLF's Budapest mentor Rudi Fischer

to Rudolph Fischer, the scholar living in Budapest who had written to him after the publication of *A Time of Gifts*. Fischer made so many valuable corrections to the book that Leigh Fermor felt he could not publish the next volume, *Between the Woods and the Water*, without consulting him in Budapest. The Fischer and Leigh Fermor friendship began in earnest when Leigh Fermor eventually wrote, asking if Fischer could possibly advise on his next volume. Typed drafts of *Between the Woods and the Water* starting appearing in brown paper parcels from Greece, which Fischer pored over with his customary meticulous scholarly attention to detail. This led to a correspondence which lasted for many years and over 400 letters, dealing with such things as Transylvanian history, customs, language, costume and legends. They contain the sort of detail extracted by James Joyce in letters from Trieste to his sister in Dublin when writing *Ulysses* in exile. He later acknowledged his debt to Fischer as 'inestimable'. He described him in a footnote to *Between the Woods and the Water* as '[t]he successor to the Polymath in *a Time of Gifts*'. They became very close friends of the sort who can play clever hoaxes on one another with no consequential ill-feeling. Before his death in 2016 Rudi Fischer solved a Leigh Fermor conundrum for me when he admitted authorship of a hoax postcard addressed to his friend in Greece from Kirchstetten, W.H. Auden's Austrian former retreat in Lower Austria. In the hoax postcard Rudi claimed it was his grandfather, 'Alois Schoissbauer', who stole Leigh Fermor's rucksack containing his money, passport and travel journal, from a Munich hostel in 1934. To add veracity to the hoax Fischer claimed the author of the postcard later inherited the rucksack and that it was stolen again by 'an Australian hippie' as he travelled across Asia to Peshawar. He signed it 'Dr Franz Xavier Hinterwalder, Professor of Farsi and Pashtoo, Firdausi School of Oriental Languages, Kirchstetten Lower Austria'. The card was written after a bibulous lunch at the Traveller's Club in Pall Mall. Leigh Fermor enjoyed the hoax card enough to copy it to Debo Devonshire.

Another reason for his return to Budapest was his wish to show the typescript to his old friend Elemér, who no doubt would have been highly amused at his own forthcoming immortalization, in a very colourful portrait, in what was to become a classic of world travel literature. Unfortunately this meeting was not to be. Leigh Fermor went to the concrete apartment block in Centenarium in Budapest's sixteenth district where he had found Elemér in 1982 but was unable to raise him by banging on the door. In a letter to Debo Devonshire he describes at length his search for his old friend. An old woman in the building indicated Elemér had been taken to hospital. He knew a young woman, who, although a Communist functionary of some sort, had taken rather a shine to the grand old man Elemér most certainly must have seemed to her. Leigh Fermor made telephone contact with her and she informed him that Elemér had been in a military hospital west of Buda. With the help of Rudi Fisher's wife Dagmar, he went to search for him. By then Elemér had been moved to an old people's' home in Pest, where he shared a room with five others. Sadly, he had slipped into another world and didn't really recognize his old friend. There were lucid moments but he kept addressing him in the third person which he found very upsetting. Leigh Fermor brought him whiskey and Earl Grey tea but Elemér was unaware that the gifts were for him. He told him his son Miklós had been to see him as had his daughter-in-law. Four months later Elemér was dead. Xenia too was dead. Being in Budapest for Leigh Fermor was by now not so much like greeting an old friend but rather saluting a memory. He left the city only returning once more in 2001 for the launch of Miklós Vajda's Hungarian translation of *Between the Woods and the Water*. The launch party was held in Buda at the Budapest Kongresszusi Központ (Budapest Congress Centre), on the occasion of the annual international Book Fair. Miklós Vajda recalled, 'Paddy came at the invitation of the publisher, Európa Könyvkiadó, headed at the time by Levente Osztovits, who liked the book very much. I spoke and introduced Paddy. The hall was packed as the publishers had done excellent advertising work.' At the event he met Katharina Hunyor, daughter of Dr Imre Hunyor of Szolnok. She brought him the family guestbook that he had signed in 1934 and there were tears of joy on both sides. 'During the following days,' Vajda recalled 'we (Paddy and I) appeared on several TV and radio programmes. One day I took him on a car trip to two cities he hadn't seen as a young man: Eger and Győr. He was especially delighted by Győr's baroque beauty.' He al-

PLF knocking on the door of 15 Úri utca.

so spent much of that visit with Rudi Fischer and his wife, Dagmar, sometimes dining in his favourite Budapest restaurant of those days, the Fekete Holló (The Black Raven) in Országház utca, a mere biscuits throw from the von Berg house in which he had stayed in 1934.

He made a symbolic, but sadly unsuccessful attempt, to gain entry to 15 Úri utca. A photograph taken by Rudi Fischer shows him knocking on the door of the house where, nearly seventy years earlier, his association with Budapest began. Sadly, there was nobody at home that day to admit him.

# Bibliography

## Archives Consulted

Bánffy Papers (in the Ráday Library), Budapest.

Barcsay Papers (in the possession of Tamás Barcsay de Nagy-Barcsa), Budapest and Toronto.

Budapest City Archives, Budapest.

Ervin Szabó Library, Budapest.

Genealogical Office, Dublin.

Historical Archives of the Hungarian State Security, Budapest.

Hungarian National Archives, Budapest.

Hunyor de Vizsoly Papers (in the possession of Katharina Hunyor de Vizsoly), Budapest.

Mátyásfalvi Collection (in the possession of János Mátyásfalvi), Budapest.

Monumente Uitate, Bucharest.

National Library of Ireland, Dublin.

Odescalchi Papers (in the possession of Prince Mark Odescalchi), Budapest and England.

Ráday Library, Budapest.

Sir Patrick Leigh Fermor Archive (Acc. 13338), National Library of Scotland, Edinburgh.

Von Berg Papers (in the possession of Baroness Gloria von Berg), Budapest.

## Printed Sources

I. Genealogical Reference Source

My constant and indispensable companion throughout the writing of this book was:

Nagy, Iván. *Magyarország családai* [Hungarian families]. Pest: Mór Ráth, 1856–68.

ll. Books by, about and related to the life of Patrick Leigh Fermor

Cooper, Artemis. *Patrick Leigh Fermor: An Adventure.* London: John Murray, 2012.

Fenwick, Simon. *Joan: The Remarkable Life of Joan Leigh Fermor.* London: Macmillan, 2017.

Fermor, Patrick Leigh. *A Time of Gifts.* London: John Murray, 1977.

Fermor, Patrick Leigh. *Between the Woods and the Water.* London: John Murray, 1986.

Fermor, Patrick Leigh. *The Broken Road.* Edited by Colin Thubron and Artemis Cooper. London: John Murray, 2014.

Mosley, Charlotte, ed. *In Tearing Haste: Letters between Deborah Devonshire and Patrick Leigh Fermor.* London: John Murray, 2008.

Sisman, Adam, ed. *Dashing for the Post: The Letters of Patrick Leigh Fermor.* London: John Murray, 2016.

lll. Books Dealing with Hungary and Transylvania Published before, around or soon after the Time of Leigh Fermor's Visit in 1934

Apponyi, Count Albert. *Lectures in the U. S. on the Peace Problems and on the Constitutional Growth of Hungary.* Budapest, 1921.

Balanyi, George. *The History of Hungary.* Budapest, 1930.

Bethlen, Count Stephen. 'Hungary in the New Europe.' *Foreign Affairs* 3.1 (1925): 445–58.

Bethlen, Count Stephen. *The Treaty of Trianon and the European Peace.* London, 1934.

Buday, László. *Dismembered Hungary.* London, 1923.

Burian, Count Stephen. *Austria in Dissolution*. New York, 1925.

Czako, Stephen. *How the Hungarian Problem Was Created*. Budapest, 1934.

Deak, Francis. *The Hungarian–Rumanian Land Dispute*. New York, 1928.

Eckhart, Francis. *A Short History of the Hungarian People*. London, 1931.

Gratz, Gusztáv. *A forradalmak kora: Magyarország története 1918–1920* [The age of revolutions: The history of Hungary, 1918–1920]. Budapest, 1935.

Great Britain, Foreign Office. *Correspondence Relative to the Affairs of Hungary, 1847–1849*. London, 1850.

*Hungarian Quarterly*, Budapest, 1936 et seq.

Jánossy, Dénes. *Great Britain and Kossuth*. Budapest, 1937.

Jaszi, Oscar. *Revolution and Counter Revolution in Hungary*. London, 1924.

Kaas, Albert. *Bolshevism in Hungary: The Béla Kun Period*. London, 1931.

Kornis, Gyula. *Education in Hungary*. New York, 1932.

Kornis, Gyula. *Hungary and European Civilization*. Budapest, 1938.

Kosary, Domokos. *A History of Hungary*. Cleveland and New York, 1941.

Lockhart, Bruce. *Seeds of War*. London, 1926.

Lukinich, Imre. *A History of Hungary*. Budapest, 1937.

Lybyer, A. Howe. *The Government of the Ottoman Empire in the Time of Suleiman the Magnificent*. Cambridge, 1913.

Macartney, C.A. *Hungary*. London, 1934.

Macartney, C.A. *Hungary and Her Successors*. Oxford, 1937.

Miller, David Hunter. *My Diary at the Conference of Paris*. Privately printed, 1928.

Nagy, Ivan. *Hungarians of the Five Hemispheres*. Budapest, 1935.

Marczali, H. 'Papers of Count Tisza, 1914–1918.' *American Historical Review* 29.1 (1924): 301–12.

Nicolson, Harold. *Peacemaking 1919*. Boston, 1933.

Riedi, Frederick. *A History of Hungarian Literature*. London, 1906.

Rutter, Owen. *Regent of Hungary.* London, 1939.

Seton-Watson. R.W. *Racial Problems in Hungary.* London, 1908.

Starkie, Walter. *Raggle-Taggle: Adventures with a Fiddle in Hungary and Roumania.* London, 1933.

Szasz, Zsombor. *The Minorities in Rumanian Transylvania.* London, 1927.

Teleki, Count Paul. *The Evolution of Hungary and Its Place in European History.* New York, 1928.

Toulmin, J. Smith. *Parallels between England and Hungary.* London, 1849.

## IV. Recently Published Works

Able Smith, Lucy. *Travels in Transylvania: The Greater Târnava Valley.* Blue Guides, London, 2nd ed 2018.

Bánffy, Miklós. *The Phoenix Land.* London: Arcadia Books, 2011.

Bánffy, Miklós. *The Transylvanian Trilogy.* London: Arcadia Books, 2009.

Barber, Annabel. *Blue Guide Budapest*, London. 2018.

Bassett, Richard. *Balkan Hours: Travels in the Other Europe.* London: John Murray, 1990.

Bassett, Richard. *For God and Kaiser: The Imperial Austrian Army.* London: Yale University Press, 2016.

Bassett, Richard. *A Guide to Central Europe.* London: Viking Press, 1987.

Blacker, William. *Along the Enchanted Way: A Romanian Story.* London: John Murray, 2009.

Carlberg, Ingrid. *Raoul Wallenberg: The Biography.* London: Maclehose Press, 2015.

Cartledge, Bryan. *The Will to Survive: A History of Hungary.* Tiverton: Timewell Press, 2006.

Clark, George B. *Irish Soldiers in Europe, 17th-19th Century.* Cork: Mercier Press, 2010.

Dent, Bob. *Budapest: A Cultural History.* Oxford: Oxford University Press, 2007.

# Bibliography

De Waal, Edmund. *The Hare with Amber Eyes*. London: Chatto & Windus, 2010.

Elsie, Robert. *Traveller, Scholar and Political Adventurer: The Memoirs of Franz Nopsca*. Budapest: Central European University Press, 2014.

Eörsi, László. *The Hungarian Revolution of 1956: Myths and Realities*. Translated by Mario D. Fenyo. Boulder, 2006.

Flaudy, György. *My Happy Days in Hell*. London: Penguin Books, 2010.

Gerő, András. *Modern Hungarian Society in the Making: The Unfinished Experience*. Translated by James Patterson and Enikő Koncz. Budapest: Central European University Press, 1995.

Hantó, Zsuzsa. *Banished Families: Communist Repression of 'Class Enemies' in Hungary*. Budapest: Magyar Ház Press, 2011.

Hoensch, Jörg K. *A History of Modern Hungary, 1867–1994*. Translated by Kim Traynor. London: Longman, 1996.

Hunt, Nick. *Walking the Woods and the Water*. London: Nicholas Brealey Publishing, 2014.

King, Charles. *Midnight at the Pera Palace: The Birth of Modern Istanbul*. New York: W.W. Norton, 2014.

Kontler, László. *A History of Hungary*. Budapest: Atlantisz, 2009.

Lukacs, John. *Budapest 1900*. New York: Grove Press, 1988.

Magris, Claudio. *Danube*. New York: Farrar Straus Giroux, 1989.

Mansel, Philip. *Constantinople*. London: John Murray, 1995.

Mari, Sándor. *Memoir of Hungary, 1944–1948*. Budapest: Corvina & Central European University Press, 2005.

Molnár, Judit. *The Holocaust in Hungary: A European Perspective*. Budapest: Balassi Press, 2015.

Molnár, Miklós. *A Concise History of Hungary*. Translated by Anna Magyar. Cambridge: Cambridge University Press, 2001.

Murphy, Dervla. *Transylvania and Beyond: A Travel Memoir*. London: John Murray, 1992.

Pálffy, Stephen. *The First Thousand Years*. Budapest: Balassi Press, 2008.

Pogany, George. *When Even the Poets Were Silent: A Jewish Hungarian Holocaust Survivor under Nazism and Communism.* London: Brandram Press, 2011.

Pratt, Michael. *The Great Country Houses of Hungary.* New York: Abbeville Press, 2007.

Pryce-Jones, David. *Unity Mitford.* London: Weidenfeld & Nicolson, 1976.

Scholten, Jaap. *Comrade Baron: A Journey through The Vanishing World of the Transylvanian Aristocracy.* Translated by Liz Waters. Saint Helena, CA: Helena History Press, 2016.

Sebestyen, Victor. *Twelve Days: Revolution 1956.* London: Weidenfeld & Nicolson, 2016.

Stone, Norman. *Turkey: A Short History.* London: Thames & Hudson, 2011.

Stone, Norman. *A Short History of Hungary.* Profile Books, 2018.

Thorpe, Nick. *The Danube: A Journey Upriver from the Black Sea to the Black Forest*, Yale UP 2013.

Török, András. *Budapest: A Critical Guide.* Budapest: Park Press, 2014.

Ungváry, Krisztián. *Battle for Budapest: 100 Days in World War II.* London: I.B. Tauris, 2014.

# Index

# Index

# Index

# Index

# Index

# Index

# Index

# Index

# Index